THE VALUES & VIRTUES BOOK

it's a God thing!

Other Books Available

The Lily Series
Here's Lily!
Lily Robbins, M.D. (Medical Dabbler)
Lily and the Creep
Lily's Ultimate Party
Ask Lily
Lily the Rebel
Lights, Action, Lily!
Lily Rules!
Rough & Rugged Lily
Lily Speaks!
Horse Crazy Lily
Lily's Church Camp Adventure
Lily's Passport to Paris
Lily's in London?!

Nonfiction
The Beauty Book
The Body Book
The Buddy Book
The Best Bash Book
The Blurry Rules Book
The It's MY Life Book
The Creativity Book
The Uniquely Me Book
The Year 'Round Holiday Book
The Values & Virtues Book
The Fun-Finder Book
The Walk-the-Walk Book
Dear Diary
Girlz Want to Know
NIV Young Women of Faith Bible
YWOF Journal: Hey! This Is Me
Take It from Me

THE VALUES & VIRTUES BOOK

it's a God thing!

Written by Nancy Rue
Illustrated by Lyn Boyer

Zonderkidz

Zonder**kidz**™

The children's group of Zondervan

www.zonderkidz.com

The Values & Virtues Book
Copyright © 2002 by Women of Faith

Requests for information should be addressed to:

Zonderkidz, *Grand Rapids, Michigan 49530*

ISBN: 0–310–70257–7

Published in association with the literary agency of Alive Communications, Inc., 7680 Goddard Street, Suite 200, Colorado Springs, CO 80920.

Editor: Barbara J. Scott
Interior design: Michelle Lenger
Art direction: Michelle Lenger
Printed in the United States of America

04 05 06/ ❖ DC/11 10 9 8 6

Contents

1.   I'm Supposed to Have Integrity?   6

2.   Integrity Makes the Grade   26

3.   Integrity Is Not a Spectator Sport   50

4.   Join the Integrity Club   68

5.   Unbreakable Faith   86

I'm Supposed to Have Integrity?

The man of integrity walks securely,
but he who takes crooked paths
will be found out.
Proverbs 10:9

Zooey sometimes feels like school is a complete waste of time. She's in what she calls the "dumb classes," and even *those* are hard for her, so she feels like an idiot for six hours every day. As if that weren't bad enough, she usually has what feels like ten tons of homework, so she gets to feel idiotic at *home* too! Zooey's solution? Pretend you don't care what grades you make. Blow off your teachers. And forget even trying to do schoolwork at home.

Suzy is really gifted at sports. She can kick tail in gymnastics, soccer, softball, *and* volleyball, and she hopes she gets a growth spurt soon so she can compete in girls' basketball too. Quiet and considerate as she is, Suzy hates to lose in any sports competition, and she'll do just about anything to win. When it looks like doing her best isn't going to be enough, she isn't willing to give up. Suzy's solution? Get away with as much stretching of the rules and dirty playing as you can, intimidate your opponents, and if you lose, sulk for days and blame it on everybody else, including your own teammates.

Reni is a natural leader, and nowhere is that more evident than in orchestra. After all, she *is* first chair violin and an All-State representative. Other kids in the orchestra tend to look up to her and see her as their spokesperson, and most of the time, Reni rises to the occasion. Sometimes, however, she rises just a little too high, becoming critical, snapping at people when they're doing stuff she considers "lame" and getting jealous when someone *else* tries to rise. Reni's solution? Remind other people just how superior she is and just how lucky they are to have her in charge. When that doesn't work, she gathers the supporters she does have and declares war.

Lily is a doer, and she goes at everything she does 100 percent and then some. She writes for the school newspaper. She's the heart and soul of the Shakespeare Club. She's the seventh grade class president. She goes out for public speaking. And that's just what she does at school. On the "outside," she does the occasional modeling gig, throws great parties, rides horses, and is involved in the junior high youth group at church. Her life is full—sometimes too full. At times she dives into things before she really knows what's in store. And sometimes she just doesn't get why the other people in these groups aren't as gung-ho as she is. Lily's solution? Try to do it all—by yourself if you have to—until you drop—or burn out—or just get so disappointed that you quit.

Kresha hangs out with the Girlz, who are a pretty spiritual group. They pray together, often go to church as a group, and for the most part try to figure out what God wants them to do in their lives. Kresha likes everything the Girlz do together, so she goes along with the God thing too. But most of the time, when she's alone, Kresha kind of figures she's got plenty of time to really be a disciple of God's son. She's young now—isn't this the time to have fun and explore her options? When anybody questions her about where she is with God, Kresha's solution is to tell them that her relationship with God is very private—and then go on about her business. But the reality is, she doesn't even have a relationship with God.

Each of our *Girlz* has a conflict, a tough situation, or a dilemma in some area of her life. Zooey struggles with school. Suzy has issues with sportsmanship. Reni is challenged when it comes to being a leader. Lily gets tangled up in the whole extracurricular activity thing. And Kresha isn't even aware that she's missing out in her relationship with God.

Even though each girl appears to be floundering in a different place, they all have one thing in common. They all need to develop *integrity*.

You may already know what integrity is or you may have heard it enough that you think it has something to do with what lawyers and doctors and judges are supposed to have. They definitely *should* have it—and so should everyone else on the face of the earth!

Integrity is a quality—just as honesty, generosity, and compassion are qualities—that every person needs to develop if she's going to be the *best* she can be at everything she does. Not the best in terms of ability—like Suzy—or natural flair—like Reni—or determination—like Lily. We're talking about being the best *person* you can be. If you have integrity, you can be the best *you* whether you win or lose, fail or succeed, excel or do your best and still barely scrape by.

"Yikes!" you may be saying. "I gotta get me some of that!"

Yes, you do—so let's find out how. We'll start with just exactly what integrity is.

The word itself really means being of sound moral principle, being upright, honest, and sincere. But it comes from a word that means complete, whole, and not easily broken apart.

In case that doesn't exactly clear things up, it might help to see the difference between what it looks like when integrity is missing and when it's a part of you.

NO INTEGRITY

Lots of Integrity

Cop an attitude in class when you don't understand the material.

Admit you're clueless and go to the teacher for help.

Take the opportunity to step on the girl on the other team when she trips and falls on the field.

Reach down and help her up.

When two of your clubs have meetings at the same time, leave one early and be late to the other one.

Decide which one you really want to go to and attend that one. Then think it over and decide if you really need to be in both.

As a group leader, don't tell those people who are un-cooperative that you're having a meeting. Maybe they'll just quit.

Give the people who don't cooperate at meetings a chance to tell you why.

When you're with people who believe in God, say you believe in Him, even though you don't, and when you're with people who don't, make fun of people who do.

Be honest about how you feel about God and then give Him at least a chance.

You've probably already figured out that integrity is something God wants us to have. Let's take a closer look at that.

How Is This a God Thing?

Time after time, Jesus told the Pharisees—who didn't have a *clue* when it came to integrity—"You are the ones who justify yourselves in the eyes of men, but God knows your hearts" (Luke 16:15).

It's that stuff "behind the appearance" that makes up your integrity. It isn't how smart you are in school—not at all. It's your attitude in class and your drive to do your best, whatever it takes. It isn't how amazing you are at sports. It's how you treat the other players and how you act when the game's over. It isn't how many clubs and activities you're involved in. It's how committed you are and how well you work with the other people who are in the activity with you. It isn't how often you go to church. It's how often you really live the faith you say you believe in.

So—you can be the *best*—even if you don't make straight As, win first-place trophies, have a different activity going on every day after school, get elected president of every club you join, or get the Sunday School attendance award five years in a row. All it takes is having the integrity to do everything completely and honestly.

In case that's still a little fuzzy around the edges for you, the Bible gives us some good examples.

When Moses was getting burned out because so many people were coming to him with their problems, his father-in-law Jethro advised him to select some men who could handle the simpler problems on the local level. He told Moses to choose men of integrity, and he spelled out integrity for him. He said that people who have integrity are those who:

- totally respect God.
- can be trusted.
- hate dishonest gain (cheaters, thieves, those kinds of folks). *(See Exodus 18:21.)*

Later, God added some additional pieces to the integrity puzzle. He said people who have integrity:

- don't twist things around to get their way.
- don't accept bribes.
- are always fair. *(See Deuteronomy 16:19–20.)*

Of course, those people back then weren't any quicker than we are, so *years* later, Micah had to tell the people again what God expected in terms of integrity. He said:

"He has showed you, O man, what is good. And what does the LORD require of you?" (Micah 6:8). He said they should:

- act justly.
- love mercy.
- walk humbly with their God.

Centuries later God was still trying to drive the point home through his son Jesus and through his servant John the Baptist. Both talked a lot about integrity. They told the people that:

- the tax collectors should not take any more money from people than they were supposed to (Luke 3:13).
- the soldiers should not blackmail people or accuse them of things they hadn't done (Luke 3:14).
- everyone should treat other people the way they themselves would want to be treated (Luke 6:31).
- they should love their enemies and pray for them (Luke 6:32–36).
- they should not pick on people, jump on their failures, or criticize their faults, but be generous with their blessings (Luke 6:37–38).

Zacchaeus should be praised for his integrity, because he gave half his income to the poor, and if he accidentally cheated anybody, he paid back four times the damages (Luke 19:8).

Jesus took Nathanael on as a disciple because he could tell just by looking at him that he didn't have a false bone in his body (John 1:47).

Finally, the idea of integrity began to stick in people's characters.

When Jesus died, a man named Joseph, who was even a member of the Jewish High Council, took Jesus' instructions so much to heart that he went to Pilate and asked for the body of Jesus. Then he prepared Jesus' body for burial and placed it in the tomb he'd installed for himself. He took a huge risk, but he did it because it was right to do (Luke 23:50–54).

When a man named Simon asked Peter to sell him the apostles' "secret" for healing people, Peter not only refused, he read the guy the riot act for trying to buy God's gift (Acts 8:18–23).

And of course Paul was all *about* integrity. When people started calling Barnabas and him "gods," Paul stopped an entire parade and set them straight, giving God all the credit for the miracles that he and Barnabas had done. (Acts 14:12–15). When he was outside of Israel, spreading the gospel, he took up a collection for the poor and brought every cent of it back with him (Acts 24:16–17). When times got hard for him and the rest of the early Christians, he didn't throw up his hands and walk off the job, nor did he try to adjust the message to make it easier so more people would join him. He just told the whole truth and let people judge for themselves (2 Corinthians 4:2).

In fact, the basic quality we have to have if we're going to live Christian lives is integrity. It's the only way, the God way, for you to be the *best you* at everything you do.

Before we talk about *how* you can get this secret ingredient, you need to take a look at where you are right now on the integrity meter. This doesn't mean you're going to find out just how rotten you really are inside! It's just a way for you to figure out where you aren't whole so you can find the right pieces that will *make* you complete.

Circle the letter of the sentence ending that sounds the *most* like what you would do in each situation. Be as *honest* as you can.

1. If my teacher made a rule that if you got caught chewing gum in class you had to stick it on your nose and leave it there for an hour, I would:

    a. never chew gum.

    b. be really careful not to get caught when I'm chewing gum.

    c. chew gum on purpose so I can refuse to stick it on my nose.

    d. complain to the teacher about the rule after school.

2. If my teacher got really sarcastic with people when they messed up doing math problems on the board, I would:

    a. work hard on my math so I won't mess up.

    b. really hope she doesn't call on me.

    c. be sarcastic right back if she pulls that on me.

    d. ask a grown-up to talk to the teacher about the way she hurts kids' feelings.

3. If we had a big, important test and I had studied all the wrong stuff, I would:

    a. tell the teacher I'm sick and can't take the test (which might actually be true when you consider how upset I'd be!).

    b. try to fake my way through it, because what else can I really do?

    c. get mad at the teacher for not being more clear about what was going to be on the test.

d. do the best I can and write a note on my paper telling the teacher what happened.

4. If I were working on a group project for school and nobody was getting the job done, I would:

a. do it all so I wouldn't get a bad grade.

b. do my part of the work and hope everybody else gets their act together.

c. refuse to do any work because I shouldn't have to if nobody else does.

d. do what I can and try to get the other people to do their parts.

5. If a class field trip was about to be canceled because somebody took the teacher's tape player, and I knew who did it, I would:

a. get the tape player from where they were hiding it and put it back on the teacher's desk when nobody is looking.

b. figure there is nothing I can do about it.

c. tell the teacher I don't think it is fair for everybody else to get punished for something one person did.

d. go to the person who took it and tell her if she doesn't return it I'll have to turn her in.

6. If I were playing in a soccer game and the referee said I fouled when I didn't, I would:

a. be sure not get anywhere close to the sidelines for the rest of the game.

b. shrug it off because, after all, it's only a game.

c. yell at the referee.

d. make sure the coach knows I didn't make the foul and then let it pass because even referees make mistakes.

7. If I were a really good softball player on a team and a friend asked me to go to a hot dog roast on the beach the night I had a practice, I would:

   a. go to the practice, but resent it the whole time.

   b. tell the coach I can't come to the practice because of family problems and then go to the hot dog roast with my friend.

   c. just not show up for practice. If I'm that good, the coach isn't going to kick me off the team.

   d. ask my friend if she'd invite me next time and then go to practice.

8. If a bunch of us in my neighborhood got together everyday after school and practiced on my trampoline in the backyard, and we were getting really good at stunts, I would:

   a. let a girl who *isn't* very good at stunts join us, even if it messes things up for the rest of us.

   b. tell a girl who isn't very good at stunts who wants to join us that my parents will only let so many people be around the trampoline at one time.

   c. make fun of a girl that isn't very good at stunts so she'll stop coming.

   d. let a girl who isn't very good at stunts stay with us and try to help her get better.

9. If I were in the Drama Club and somebody else got the part in a play that I wanted really badly, I would:

   a. do an incredible job at the small part I did get so the teacher will wish she'd picked me for the big part.

b. do okay at the small part I got and hope the girl who got the role I wanted will get sick or break a leg or something.

c. tell everybody the girl who got my part thinks she's all that.

d. do a great job with my small part so the whole play will be good.

10. If I'd been taking dance since I was five and I was really tired of it, I would:

a. keep taking lessons because my parents have put a lot of money and time into it.

b. stop giving it my best and hope the teacher will tell my parents I need to quit.

c. flat out tell my parents I plan to quit.

d. talk it over with my parents and my dance teacher.

11. If I were president of a club and I had a great idea I wanted the club to do but some people didn't want to do it, I would:

a. give up the idea and do what they want to do.

b. get together with the people who like my idea and just do it with them.

    c.   tell them too bad because I'm the leader so I have the final say.

    d.   discuss it with the whole group and see if we can come up with a compromise.

12. If people made fun of me for closing my eyes and saying a silent prayer before I ate my lunch in the school cafeteria, I would:

    a.   stop praying before I eat.

    b.   pray without closing my eyes or bowing my head.

    c.   tell them they aren't going to heaven because *they* don't pray.

    d.   ask them to stop—and then silently pray for *them*.

13. If I were at a youth rally and everybody else was really getting into the praise music (waving arms, dancing around, closing their eyes and tilting their faces up) and I wasn't, I would:

    a.   pretend I am into it too.

    b.   escape to the restroom.

    c.   goof around and mimic the people who are into it.

    d.   just do what I am moved to do as I sing.

Count how many you circled of each letter and put the numbers in these slots:

"a"   2

"b"   0

"c"   0

"d"   9

    Before we tell you what these numbers may mean for you, remember that the purpose of checking yourself out is to find out where you are, so you will know what to do to improve your sense of integrity.

If you have more a's than other letters, you might think of yourself as a person with a lot of integrity because you like to make everything right. Sometimes that does prove your integrity—when you study hard for a test, work on your soccer dribbling, try to get every badge in Girl Scouts, and memorize more Bible verses than anybody in the whole Sunday school—as long as you're doing it all for the right reasons. What would the *wrong* reasons be? How about these:

- because you want people to think you're wonderful
- because you don't want to hurt anybody's feelings
- because you don't like conflict or arguments
- because you don't think it's okay to have a mind of your own

As you read this book, we hope you'll find out that integrity is about being real as well as good. And never fear—we're going to show you how to *get* real too.

If you have more b's than other letters, you may sometimes be a little more interested in not getting caught doing something wrong than you are in actually doing what's right. That doesn't make you a horrible person! It does mean that as you read this book, you'll want to pay attention to what we have to say about *doing* what is good instead of just *knowing* what is good. You've got that part down, so you're halfway there already! We'll take you the rest of the way.

If you have more c's than other letters, you may have an attitude hurdle you'll want to kick out of the way! It's just hard for you not to get your own way or be in charge, and a lot of times that keeps you from exercising your integrity instead of your mouth. But don't toss this book in the trash and say, "That's tough! It's just the way I am!" Your energy, your ability to speak out, even your general bull-headedness can serve you well if you use them the right way—with integrity. Read on. We're going to show you how.

If you have more d's than other letters—and you chose those answers honestly and not just because you figured they were the "right" ones—you *know* what's right and you will *do* what's right, not only because it *is* right but because you *want* to do what's right. (Whew!) That doesn't mean you've got it all together and can now just pass this book on to someone else. Knowing you can always be better than you are right now is part of integrity too. Read with an open mind. You're going to learn some things you don't already know about keeping your sense of integrity strong even when it isn't popular.

Just Do It

There are three activities below. Give each of them a try (your *best* try, of course!)

1. Start by trying to see yourself the way God sees you. Look in the mirror and say something positive to yourself, something you really mean about what you see there. Say it out loud. Say it everyday for five days in a row.
2. Now see what it feels like to act with integrity. Think of one thing about your character that you don't like. (For example, maybe you tend to sit back and let other people do all the work.) Then think of one thing you could do that is the opposite of that (like offer to do your brother or sister's chore tonight). Now just do it.
3. And now, see how other people react when you treat them with integrity. Think of somebody who does things for you that you pretty much take for granted—like your mom doing your laundry or your teacher giving you extra help in language arts. Think of something you could do for that person to show your appreciation—like hugging your mom and thanking her for the clean socks, or taking your teacher some of those jelly beans you've been hoarding.

Girlz WANT TO KNOW

✿ *ZOOEY: This sounds really cool, building up my integrity, but I'm afraid I'll get started doing the activities and stuff, and then I'll just quit. I do that a lot. My mom says I never finish anything.*

Zooey, try looking at it as making a promise. Don't you hate it when somebody tells you she's going to do something—like call you or meet you someplace—and then she doesn't come through? When you set out to improve your sense of integrity, it might help to think of it as keeping a promise to yourself. You know how you're going to feel if you don't keep that promise, because it's the same way you feel when other people don't come through for you. Try practicing keeping promises to yourself so you can learn to trust yourself. Try these steps:

- Right now, identify one thing that needs to be done today that you haven't gotten around to. Just *one thing*—like picking your dirty clothes up off the floor and taking them to the laundry room or studying for your spelling test and asking someone to call out the words to you. Then do it right away or set a specific time when you can later.

- Next, identify one thing you'd like to do for yourself but you've been too lazy or too timid to try. Just *one thing*—like putting on your in-line skates after school (instead of watching television) and practicing some moves in the driveway. Then do it right now or set a specific time when you can do it later.

When you've kept those two promises to yourself, reward yourself. Take a bubble bath or paint your toenails with glittery polish or enjoy a honkin' huge piece of bubble gum.

Repeat that process everyday. Keep one promise to yourself at a time.

✿ *RENI: The thing I'm worried about with this whole integrity thing is that I have a lot of integrity—at least I think I do—but I'm not always that nice to other people when I'm doing the right thing. Like when somebody does something rude, I'll say, "Man, Zooey, that was pretty evil!" You know, stuff like that.*

Sometimes you have to be the bad guy in order to do the right thing—but not always. The thing you probably need to work on is kindness. That doesn't mean always saying sweet, adorable things to people. It means thinking of integrity as doing small acts of kindness rather than just acting as "The Enforcer." Try this:

- Sometime today, do a kind thing for somebody, only don't let anyone know you're doing it. Slip into your mom and dad's room and make their bed for them. Stick an unsigned note in someone's math book that says, "I think you're cool." Put a Hershey's kiss on your teacher's desk when he or she isn't looking.

- Sometime today, do a kind thing for somebody you don't even know. Let a kid go ahead of you in the lunch line. Warn a girl in the restroom that there's no toilet paper in that stall she's going into. Hold the door open for the old lady going into the video store.

Do one of each of these things everyday. Be conscious of it. It will soften you and help you to be kind in your acts of integrity, rather than just standing for *might* and *right*.

❁ *SUZY: I feel guilty a lot—I mean, really bad—because I do and think so many things that don't have integrity in them. I'm afraid if I try to improve, I'm just going to feel worse!*

Wow, Suzy, it sounds like you're really beating yourself up, and you don't need to do that. God doesn't punish us for every little rotten thing we do, so why should we do that to ourselves? Try being more gentle with yourself by:

- not expecting yourself to be perfect.
- laughing at the stupid things you do!
- forgiving yourself when you mess up.
- learning from your mistakes and moving on.

Try this for one day: Every time you catch yourself putting yourself down for something you've done or thought or said ("It was bad of me to think Lily is bossy." "I shouldn't have butted in when Reni was talking." "I should be happier about doing the dishes for Mom.") go ahead and own up to it, but then think three positive things about yourself. ("I try not to hurt people's feelings." "I usually give other people a chance to talk." "I do my chores everyday whether I want to or not.") Pretty soon you'll learn to give yourself a break. You'll make a lot more progress in changing that way.

❁ *LILY: I totally want to have more integrity, and I can't wait to get started. Only it's the same old thing—my family's gonna say, "Here we go again. Lily's got a new thing." I hate that.*

Yeah, that's pretty low when people make fun of you for trying to be a better person. However, this is one of those things you can do without making it public. Integrity is all about *not* telling everybody you have it! So just go along doing the activities and watch your integrity grow—just don't advertise it at the dinner table. If you do get frustrated because your little brother makes fun of you for helping your mom without being asked, or something like that, you need an *escape route*.

Choose a place where you can go, an activity you can do, that helps you shake off the frustrations and the itchies and the little things that needle you. Can you  lock yourself in your room and play your favorite music? Escape to the basement and beat up the punching bag? Flop into the hammock and vent to the clouds? Go down to the park and swing on the swings like there's no tomorrow? It's a good thing to learn how to do, because no matter how much integrity you have, the world isn't always going to see things your way. Don't you hate *that*?

Talking to God About It

Dear __God__ *, (your favorite way of addressing God)*
I'm thinking I need to work on my integrity so I can be the best me at everything I do, because right now, I'm not in such a good place. When it comes to integrity, God, I see myself as
__not to wraped up in grades__.
So will you please help me to get past that? There are gonna be some obstacles. So please help me with the ones I've checked off here, (as well as the ones you know about that I haven't even thought of!):

_____ *I feel dumb at school.*
_____ *I hate school.*

_____   *I'm bored at school.*

_____   *I get frustrated with teachers and rules and stuff like that.*

✓   *I don't like it when kids make fun of me.*

_____   *I don't get along with some kids.*

_____   *I don't want to be around some kids who want to hang with me.*

✓   *I feel like I always have to win.*

_____   *I get mad when other people don't help the team.*

_____   *I'm tired of doing stuff after school.*

✓   *I wish I were in more activities after school.*

✗   *I wish I were in different activities after school.*

_____   *I don't feel like anyone listens to my ideas.*

√√√   *I sometimes get bossy.*

✓   *I sometimes go for a whole day without even thinking about you.*

_____   *I wish my parents would take me to church.*

_____   *I don't like my church.*

_____   *I don't see what good it does to pray.*

✓   *I don't like how some kids make fun of me because I pray.*

    Please, God, clear my path and guide me along the way. If I stumble, pick me up and help me get going again, especially when:

_____   *I don't see any changes right away.*

✓   *I get tired of being so good when nobody else seems to care about being good.*

_____   *I think of something that would be more fun to do than being good.*

_____   *I feel somebody pulling me in the wrong direction.*

    Thanks, God, for giving me the chance to be all you want me to be. I know since you want that, you'll do all you can to help me. Please help me to remember that.

    I love you—

Katie pride

The person I know with the most integrity is ...

Kali. She loves to win but also loves when her opponet win. she does her best even if it isn't the teacher's best. She isn't afraid to ask for help. and is very kind. she laphs alot !! She is who she says she is!

Integrity Makes the Grade

**Hold on to instruction, do not let it go;
guard it well, for it is your life.**

Proverbs 4:13

Did you just read that Bible verse? Did it actually say instruction is your *life*?

If you're like a lot of kids, you sure *hope* not! You are definitely holding out hope that there is more to life than going to school. After all, almost every person between grades one and twelve has *some* kind of issue with education.

Lily freaks if she doesn't get straight A's—and not just on her report card. She wants an A on every assignment, from pop quizzes to major projects.

Reni gets annoyed with the other kids in her classes because they mess around so much. School for her wouldn't be so bad if she weren't surrounded by "losers."

Suzy has trouble with all the rules. It isn't that she doesn't agree with them—it's just that there are so many of them. She's terrified she's going to break one and end up in the office getting suspended.

Zooey gets sick of feeling "dumb." Her teachers don't help her—they just point out that if she worked harder and paid closer attention she'd make better grades. Well, duh! Don't they know she's *tried* that?

Kresha just doesn't see what good all the stuff she's studying in school is ever going to do her. She doesn't care about the exports of Peru or numbers to the tenth power. She's thinking she wants to be a mechanic, so who needs all that garbage?

Maybe you have similar gripes about school. If adults—even teachers!—are honest, they'll admit that in some cases you actually have a point. It really would help if everybody cooperated in class, if there weren't the need for so many rules and regulations, and if kids who struggle could get all the help they needed. There's nothing wrong with trying to get those things changed, but in the meantime, they're things you pretty much have to deal with to get an education. The one thing you *can* change is your attitude toward the things that drive you stark-raving mad. An attitude that's going to work for you comes from—big surprise—having integrity.

Of course, if you don't *want* to change your attitude because, frankly, you couldn't care *less* about getting an education—that's something else entirely. Let's start our discussion of how to be the *best you* in school by looking at God's view of education.

HOW IS THIS A God Thing?

If it makes you feel any better, kids have been asking why they have to go to school and study since Bible days. Otherwise, why would there be so many verses telling them they have to listen, pay attention, study, and work hard? If they'd *wanted* to do it, nobody would have had to tell them all that! The Book of Proverbs is loaded with "strong suggestions" for kids about learning:

"Listen, my sons [and it goes for daughters too], to a father's instruction; pay attention and gain understanding. I give you sound learning, so do not forsake my teaching" (Proverbs 4:1–2). This particular father goes on to inform his kids that *his* father had to tell him the same things when *he* was a kid.

"Get wisdom," he continues. "Get understanding; do not forget my words or swerve from them" (Proverbs 4:5). By now, these kids are thinking, "Yeah, yeah, we've heard this before." But the dad goes on: "Listen, my son, accept what I say, and the years of your life will be many." He's not talking about making good grades in school. He's talking about getting an education so you can stay *alive*! This man is serious! As well he should be—and so should you—because just as it was back then, your education is a *huge* part of your future.

Now, before you start waving this book around and saying, "The future? I'm *ten*, for Pete's sake!" we're not talking about your ability to get a job or have a career, although that's part of what a good education can do for you. We're talking about training your mind, getting it into good shape, so that it can do anything it's required to do in this life. Like Kresha, you may be wailing that none of the stuff you're learning has anything to do with the life you want to live. But in *every* life, a person needs to be able to:

- focus on important things without getting distracted every seven seconds.
- put pieces of things together in your head so they make sense as a whole (which is called synthesizing) so that, for instance, you can plan a party or a vacation or gather information to make a decision.
- write so people can read what you're thinking.
- speak so people can understand what you're saying.
- create—anything!
- analyze—so you can buy a car, raise a kid, figure out what the Bible is talking about!
- explore—mountains, malls, options.
- imagine—whatever you want.

The list actually goes on, but you get the idea. If your mind isn't trained to do those things, they aren't just going to happen automatically. Without the ability to focus, synthesize, analyze, and so on, not only will you end up doing a boring job day after day for the rest of your *life,* but you'll also end up having to take whatever comes along in the other areas of your life as well—like where you go, who you hang out with, where you live, even how you relate to God. Yes, God loves the person with a second-grade education as much as he loves the woman with the Ph.D.—but the person with only a second-grade education won't be able to read about the experiences of other Christians, won't be equipped to go out and do mission work, won't be able to make great ideas for the church happen.

An education teaches you to think in every way possible so all your life you can keep learning—and what you'll learn won't *always* have to be about the exports of Peru—unless, of course, that fascinates you.

There's one more thing. When that father in Proverbs says, "Pay attention to my wisdom, listen well to my words of insight, . . . that your lips may preserve knowledge" (Proverbs 5:1–2), it isn't just a fancy way of saying, "Shut up and listen to me, kid, maybe you'll learn something." He's saying, "Learn, because it's going to be up to you to pass all this good stuff on to *other* people."

The education you're getting isn't just so you can have a great life—although that's nice too. Part of the job God put each of us here to do is to share the God thing with other people. It doesn't matter whether you do it as a missionary teaching in Zimbabwe or as a plumber praying for every person whose toilet she unclogs, your job is to share. It's tough to do that if you can't focus, synthesize, speak, analyze—well, you get the idea.

Education is a God thing. Ya gotta go for it.

CHECK Yourself OUT

It's all very well and good to say God wants you to have an education, but that doesn't erase all the problems kids have with school. That's where more attitude stuff comes in.

Let's take a few minutes here to check out what your current attitude is toward education—whether you're in a public school, a private academy, or a home school situation. Remember—as *always*—that this "quiz" is not to determine how "good" or "bad" your attitude is. Right now, it just is what it is—and that's what we need to find out before we move on.

Choose the answer in each set below which best describes how you *feel*—not what you know is right or what you think is probably true. Go by what you feel, just this once. (Remember that going by your feelings isn't always the best way to make a decision, but we need to pay attention to them so they can point us to *what* decisions we have to make in the first place.)

1. When it's time to get out of bed to go to school:

    a. I can't wait to get up and get ready.

    b. I would rather sleep some more, but once I'm up it's not so bad.

    c. I would rather be shot.

2. The thing I love most about school is:

   (a.) everything.

   b. lunch, recess, and going home.

   c. absolutely nothing.

3. I think my teacher is:

   (a.) amazing.

   (b.) okay, I guess.

   c. the enemy.

4. The assignments I enjoy most are the ones where:

   (a.) I get to be creative and use my own ideas.

   b. I don't have to think that much, like filling in blanks on sheets.

   c. Enjoy myself? You're kidding, right?

5. To me, the rules in school are:

   (a.) okay. I just don't break them.

   b. kind of stupid, but I can sometimes get around them.

   c. completely lame. I'm always getting in trouble because I don't follow them.

6. I'm sure my teacher thinks I am:

   (a.) a really good student.

   b. an okay student but not as good as I could be if I tried harder.

   c. a pain in the neck.

7. I would like school a lot better if:

   a. we got to do more neat, creative projects instead of so many worksheets.

b. we studied more things I cared about.

c. we didn't have to go at all.

8. School makes me feel like I can:

a. grow up to be just about anything I want.

b. hardly wait to get out so I can do what I want.

c. not do a single thing right.

9. As far as my future goes, I think school is:

a. very important.

b. something I have to put up with so I won't wind up being dumb.

c. a total waste of time.

10. If only my teacher wasn't so:

a. busy with the kids that mess around all the time.

b. demanding, expecting me to be perfect.

c. mean and unfair to me.

Count your a's, b's, and c's and put the numbers in the slots below.

"a" 8

"b" 2

"c" 0

Below you'll find explanations of what your scores *may* mean. Keep two things in mind as you read:

1. Read *all* the explanations, even if you had *no* answers in a particular category. You'll probably see a little of yourself in each one.

2. Remember that your highest score doesn't put you in a slot. The explanation is just here to help you see that you're not the only one who feels that way, and that the way you feel can change for the better.

If you had more a's than other letters, that *probably* means you like school most of the time. You especially like it when you can be creative and really use your mind and your own ideas. Chances are you're in a class where you get to do a lot of that kind of thing, which is part of why you have the excited attitude you have. If you're a person reading this who loves the creative projects but hates school, it's probably because you're not being given the chance to learn in the way that's the most satisfying for you.

Read on—we can help you deal with that. In fact, everyone should go ahead and read on, because no matter how much you adore going to school (Okay—that might be a little strong!), there are bound to be parts of it that don't excite you. Some attitude adjustment—some integrity—can really help you deal with those rough spots.

If you had more b's than other letters, that *may* mean that you don't exactly hate school, but a lot of the time it's pretty boring for you, which tends to keep you from doing your best. That's a bummer, because there are definitely teachers out there who don't exactly know how to make education an adventure! But that doesn't mean you have to snooze your way through to your senior year. Read on. We can help you conquer the boredom with a different attitude. It's all about integrity, girl.

If you had more c's than other letters, that *could* mean school is the worst thing *about* your life and you would rather eat brussels sprouts daily for the rest of your life than spend another day in that classroom. As a result, you probably get into hot water with your teachers and parents a lot. You may not be the class behavior problem, throwing spit wads and smart-mouthing the teacher, but you more than likely get "yelled at" for not turning in assignments or for doing them only halfway or for daydreaming when you're supposed to be working. It's probably a miracle that you're reading this chapter at all—but hang in there! Help is on its way. We may not be able to change a lot about school, but we can change you—and you are half your education. Keep reading!

Just Do It

Because the very best way to learn is to *do*, we're going to help you understand attitude and integrity in school by asking you to *do* some things. Your results are going to teach you much more than any written explanation could. (You get enough of that in school, right?)

The first set of **Just Do It** activities is for everybody, to help you understand the basics of school integrity. Then you'll find a second set where you can choose the activities that fit your special 'tude challenges.

SET I. Do *all* of these activities. Feel free to stretch them out over a couple of days. Don't rush. The idea is to *do* and then realize what you've learned.

1. Try this experiment. (It's just an experiment. We don't suggest you go at school this way everyday!) For one day at school, pretend you totally love everything about it. Make a game of it (but don't let anyone else know you're just pretending). Act like you're delighted with every assignment. Pretend the food in the cafeteria is delicious. Behave as if your teacher is your favorite person on earth. If you've always liked school, think of the things that you aren't crazy about when it comes to your school day and pretend you *do* like that particular thing (boys acting like morons on the playground, no paper towels in the restrooms, etc.) When you go home that afternoon, go to a quiet place and think back over the day. Was there anything different about your day besides the way *you* were acting? Did anybody treat you differently? Was the work the same as always? Did you feel the same as usual? Write down the differences—if there were any—on these lines:

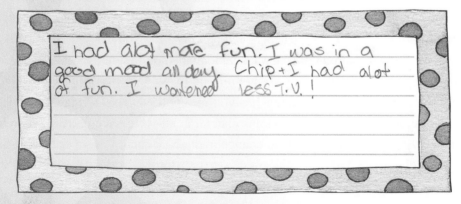

I had alot more fun. I was in a good mood all day. Chip + I had alot of fun. I watched less T.V.!

2. On a different day, try this experiment. Think of one thing you *do* like about school. If you love school, think of the thing you love most. If you think you hate everything about school, challenge yourself to dig in there and find some little tidbit (anything except "When we get to go home" or "When we get a day off"). Once you've picked your "thing," try to fit it into your day as much as you can.

If you like it that the teacher lets you read anything you want when you get your work done, whip through those assignments so you get a ton of reading time. If recess is your favorite thing, keep yourself going by looking forward to it, and then make it the best recess on record, enjoying every second of it. If the only thing you can get jazzed about is when you get to do art, get your other work done and then ask the teacher if you can work on an art project. If that doesn't work, you could go to the library and get some art books or just draw at your desk until the next assignment. At the end of the day, decide which one of these categories the day fits into. Was it:

_____ better than most of my days at school.

_____ about the same as most of my days at school except for

_____.

_____ exactly the same as every other day in school.

_____ worse than most days at school.

3. On still another day, choose the thing you *dislike* the most about school. If you like just about everything, pick something that occasionally gets on your nerves. If you think you despise absolutely everything, narrow it down to the hateful thing at the top of your list.

Once you've got that one thing firmly in mind, go to school and observe it as if it were the subject of a science experiment—as if it were something you were watching from outside a fish tank or test tube. Write down the things you observe as you go (but get your work done first, of course). For example, if you can't stand your teacher—can't *stand* her!—observe her for the day as if you were in another room watching her through a window, hearing her voice on a speaker. Respond when she calls on you, of course, but the rest of the time, just watch her carefully.

36

If the thing you're observing is not getting to go to the bathroom when you need to—having to wait until it's "bathroom time"—watch that whole process as if you were assessing it for some serious study you had to report to someone. Take careful notice of how it feels to be squirming in your seat, how the other kids seem to be handling the situation, what goes on in the line when you finally do get to file to the restroom. When you go home that afternoon, find a quiet place and look at your notes or think back over the day. Then see if you can answer the following questions, either in writing or just in your head:

1. What is it exactly that you don't like about this thing? Break it down into the specific things that bug you. (Example: The teacher doesn't give you a chance to explain. She doesn't give you enough time to finish your assignments. She's always in a hurry, even when you want to tell her something cool. She never has time to listen.)

   _____

2. While observing your hateful thing from the outside, was there any stuff that really doesn't seem so bad now? (Example: She really doesn't raise her voice that much.)

   _____

3. Is there any part of this hateful thing that you could possibly change? Even just a little? (Example: Choosing a better time to tell your teacher "cool stuff" when you can see that she's busy grading papers or writing something on the board.)

   _____

We'd love it if you learned something from your experiments. Hopefully, your conclusions included these important 'Tude Changers:

Tude Changer #1: Be as positive as you can possibly be. That doesn't mean you should sit there grinning like a goon when you're actually miserable. Just try to see the up side of things, and about 50 percent of the time, you'll get more "up" responses from other people, including that wretched teacher (who will probably be 50 percent less wretched!).

Tude Changer #2: Find your niche. A niche is that comfortable spot where you feel confident and strong and interested. You can't always be in that niche, but be there as much as you can without neglecting the other not-so-nichey stuff you have to do. If you have at least one thing at school that you're good at and enjoy, doing that *will* make the rest of the day go better—guaranteed.

Tude Changer #3: **You can't change everything, but you can change some things.** Most of the time when we're completely unhappy in a situation, we haven't looked for what we can do to make at least part of that situation bearable. So maybe you hate it that you can't run to the restroom whenever you need to, but you can decide not to drink three glasses of milk at breakfast or ask your mom to write the teacher a note saying you have special bladder needs. When you take action to change the things that *can* be changed, it will be easier for you to accept the things you *can't* do anything about.

SET II. Do only those activities below that fit you. These aren't one-time exercises; they're actions you'll need to take over and over again until they become part of the way you naturally think and behave. Do only one activity at a time. Nobody can change everything at once!

❀ *RENI: What if I'm completely bored in school?*

- Remember that sometimes you just have to plow through boring stuff. That's life. Not everything is going to be fascinating (just ask your parents next time you see them scrubbing the toilets or reading the same book to your little brother for the forty-millionth time!)
- Make a list of the things that do interest you in school. Think of absolutely everything. Then think of everything else you do in school as just stuff you have to put up with so you can also do the good stuff.
    - If you're bored when you're the first one to finish that math sheet, ask your teacher if there are some math puzzles or games you could do while you're waiting for everybody else to finish.
    - Take every opportunity you can to do what *does* interest you. Pick your favorite books when it's time for book

reports. If you're an artist, illustrate your essays. If you're into dolls, do your next social studies report on how dolls have developed through the centuries. If all you want to do is play soccer, write about it, read about it, or talk about it whenever an assignment offers a choice of subject.

- Ask your parents if you can take special classes in the things you're into—as long as you keep up with your schoolwork too.
- Remember that most of the time, it's up to *you* to make your life interesting.
- If you truly feel that you're bored because the work is too easy for you, ask your parents to talk to your teacher.

✿ *ZOOEY: The work in school is way hard for me.*

- Do *not* think of yourself as stupid! We all have learning abilities, but we also learn in different ways. Many teachers only teach to one type of learner. Once you find out how you learn best, things are going to get easier. So everyday, pray that God will help you *not* to think of yourself as the biggest moron on the planet.
- Ask yourself this: If a friend were going to give you directions to her house, which of these ways would you like her to use to give you those instructions?

   a. Write them in words on a piece of paper.
   b. Draw a map for you.
   c. Tell you the directions.
   d. Take you there one time so you could find it alone the next time.

If you chose **a,** you are probably a **verbal** learner. Words make sense to you, especially when you read them. When you don't understand something in school, ask your teacher to write down the instructions or the explanation for you or show you where you can find them in your book or workbook. Read them over and over. You'll get it.

If you chose **b,** you are more than likely a **visual** learner. You learn best from diagrams and pictures. When you don't understand something in school, ask your teacher to show you with props or a sketch. (When you learned about addition, did the teacher hold up one ball and then another and ask you how many you had when you put them together? That's visual learning.) Keep the diagram or picture in front of you. It will really help.

If you chose **c,** there's a good chance you are an **audio** learner. That means you learn best when you hear instructions or explanations. You are probably a person who can go to a movie once and almost recite the dialogue from memory. You learn the words to songs after hearing them only a few times. If you don't understand something in school, ask your teacher to read the instructions out loud to you or explain it to you in her own words if you can't get them from reading them off a page. Most of the time, that's all it takes to make things clearer to you.

If you chose **d,** it's a safe bet you learn best by *doing*—you are a **hands-on** learner. If you can just do a thing one time, it's there in your mind forever. You may have learned to ride a two-wheeler right off the bat. You're probably the person in the family who knows how to program the VCR or get the printer to work on the computer. The problem for you is that a lot of what you're expected to learn in school isn't taught that way—but don't despair. If you don't understand something, ask your teacher to "walk you through it" step-by-step. Whether it's doing long division or diagramming sentences, you can do it if someone guides you through it the first few times.

Teachers are very busy and don't always have a chance to work with people individually in class, so if you're having trouble, show this section to your parents so that they'll know the best way to help you at home.

Sometimes other kids can explain things in a way that makes sense to another kid! Pick out a student in your class who seems to understand the thing you're struggling with and ask him or her to help you.

Above all, don't give up! You are not a hopeless case. There *is* a way for you to learn what you need to learn. And you're still young—even though we're encouraging you to take some responsibility for your education, most of it is still up to the adults in your life. Talk honestly to your parents about your problems in school. Show them how hard you're trying. They love you—of course they'll help you.

❀ *KRESHA: I just can't keep it all together in school. I'm always forgetting to do something, and I can never find my papers.*

The solution to your problem is a matter of getting organized. Of course, if you knew how to get organized, you wouldn't be in this mess in the first place! Try these tips to get you on track:

- Ask someone to help you make a checklist of all the things you generally need to take to school with you. (Lunch, backpack, homework, soccer ball, etc.) Post your checklist near the door you use most and check it every morning before you leave for school. At first, the trick is going to be remembering to check the checklist, so ask somebody in your family to remind you for a while (probably not your mom, who may already be thinking for three or four people).
- Ask your teacher or some really organized kid in your class (you know the one—she always has sharpened pencils in her pencil case and her crayons are never broken) to go through your book bag or backpack with you and help you get organized. (Don't have a bag or pack? Uh—that's a must. No wonder your stuff is scattered all over the globe!)
- Chances are your backpack isn't going to stay neatly organized, so you'll have to go through that same drill at least once a week. Make it a fun time. Turn on your favorite music or tune in to a TV show or video you like. Fix a bowl of popcorn. Spread out on the floor and clean house in your backpack. Once you've done that two weeks in a row, it will start to become a habit—a *good* habit!

- When your teacher puts assignments on the board or tells them to the class, *write them down!* And not just on any old sheet of paper. Get yourself a cool little notebook—one you've decorated yourself in some cool way. Use that amazing gel pen that writes in green ink only for your assignments. If you're not getting it together at first, ask your teacher to check your list for you before you leave. When you get home, whip out that assignment notebook and go down the list as you do your homework. Give yourself stickers or stars or stamps when you complete them. (And don't forget to put the notebook back in your backpack). Make the process as much fun for yourself as you can.

  - If that doesn't work, talk to your parents about asking the teacher to send home an assignment sheet with you for a while, until you get the hang of being organized.

✿ *SUZY: I get really nervous about some things in school, like taking tests or talking in front of the class.*

That's what we call anxiety, and it can be almost sickening. When you suffer from test anxiety, everything leaves your mind, and you can hardly pick up your pencil. When you have "stage fright," your knees wobble, your teeth chatter, and you're sure if you open your mouth, not one single word is going to come out. It's very real and needs very real attention.

- Prepare as well as you can for every test or oral report or speech you have to give. Good preparation helps relieve the jitters. Know your material so well, you can almost write it down or present it like you're on automatic pilot.
- Practice taking tests and giving speeches at home, where you're relaxed. Part of the fear is the unknown—and if you've been there and done that, the fear tends to fade some.

- Let your teacher know that you suffer from anxiety. Every educator wants to know everything about each student, especially things that affect performance in the classroom. Don't be embarrassed about it—it happens to more people than you realize.
- Before you have to take a test or stand up in front of the class, close your eyes and imagine yourself doing what you have to do. Picture every detail in your mind.
- When you feel anxiety mounting up (butterflies in your stomach, palms getting clammy, hands shaking), close your eyes and take several deep breaths.
- Pray. Talk to God a *lot* about your fears. Pray while you're preparing. Pray while the tests are being handed out. Pray when you're called on. God does *not* want you to be afraid!
- Let fear give you energy. The thing that makes your mouth go dry and your hands sweat is a hormone called adrenaline. It sounds like a bad thing, but it's also the body juice that helps you run fast when you're being chased! It's energy, so let it brighten your eyes and give life to your voice when you're speaking. Let it move your hand lickety-split across the page when you're writing down those answers.
- If your anxiety is so bad that it paralyzes you and you absolutely cannot write or speak or think, talk seriously to your mom and dad about it. Ask them to consult with your teacher and maybe the school counselor. It isn't enough to say, "There's nothing to be afraid of." Obviously, your body is telling you there *is*, and there are real pros in the schools who can help you overcome that fear.

✿ *ZOOEY: I make promises to myself and my mom that I'm really going to try to do better and then I don't.*

That's probably because your motivation—the reason that drives you to do something—is coming from outside of you instead of inside. A promise is just words if there isn't a good reason behind it—a reason you really believe in. Think about it this way: if your dad says you're not to talk longer than twenty minutes on the phone or you're going to be punished, you will more than likely not break that rule when he's at home—but what if you're home alone? Whether you obey the rule depends on your motivation—what's going on inside you that determines what you really *want* to do. It's the same with promises about school. If you don't really *want* to do well in school, you won't, no matter how many promises you make. So how do you get motivated? Try this:

• Think of one thing that really interests you—one thing that you get jazzed about when you do it or hear about it or see it on TV. It could be animals, sports, clothes, ballet—whatever. Write it here:

  singing + danceing

• Now make a list of all the skills you need in order to do or learn about that thing. For example, if it's training dogs, you have to be able to read, observe behavior, discipline yourself (as well as the dog!), and speak clearly. Write the skills needed to become an expert in your "thing" here:

  listen well/*controled movements*
  ☆ a stage fright

• Now look at that list of skills and put a star next to each one that you can work on in school. From the dog-training list, you would probably put a star next to: read, discipline yourself, and speak clearly.

• For the next five days in school, keep a list of those skills on a small piece of paper or card on your desk or in your pocket. Look at it every time you think about it. See how often you're doing schoolwork that actually helps you develop those skills. Yeah, you may be reading some "lame" thing about how your digestive system works (yuck!) but at least you're practicing reading so you can read more advanced stuff about dog training later. Besides, who knows when info about digestive systems could come in handy with your pup?

❀ *LILY: Sometimes people call me a nerd or a weirdo because I actually like to study and learn.*

That is a complete bummer. It probably doesn't help to know that people do that because (1) they're jealous or (2) they feel like they're not as smart as you are and that sort of scares them or (3) they don't understand you because they hate school and studying, and some people tend to lash out at what they don't understand. But go ahead and pray for those people anyway (Jesus said we have to), and then try these things to take the sting out of those comments:

- Don't expect everybody to love the whole learning thing as much as you do, because everybody isn't made that way. And definitely don't act superior to people who would just as soon be watching "I Love Lucy" reruns on TV. Sometimes people poke fun at other people because they think *those* people are putting *them* down, just by the look on their faces.
- Find other students who are learning buffs like you are and make friends with them. There has to be another kid who digs math or gets lost for hours in the outer space website or likes to put on costumes and play Robin Hood or Camelot. Those people aren't going to put you down, because they know what it's like, and they're going to think you're cool!
- Give yourself plenty of un-ridiculed time to pursue your learning interests. Read your books, search the Internet, decorate eighteenth century dollhouses, or pretend you're a pioneer woman when there's nobody around to tell you that you aren't normal. That will reassure you that it's okay to just be who you are and allow you to enjoy being that person.
- Find out what the other kids in your class who don't get labeled "nerds" are interested in and don't blow it off as being beneath you! In other words, don't be a snob. So maybe video games seem like a waste of time to you, but have you ever tried one? Maybe you think it's absurd to spend your allowance on Barbie paraphernalia, but have

you ever actually explored the Barbie aisle at Toys 'R Us? True learners are always open to new things. Don't knock it unless you've tried it (except of course for stuff that *nobody* should be trying!).

❁ *KRESHA: I really don't hate the work all that much, but I just have trouble sitting still and being quiet for as long as I have to in school.*

You're a person who has a ton of energy (has your mom ever told you she'd like to have about half of it herself?), and you just need to find ways to use it up so you aren't busting out of your seat. Here are a few suggestions:

• Get as much exercise as you can when you aren't in the classroom. Run around at recess. Do jumping jacks in the restroom.

• Make sure you're doing active things after school and at home. Are you involved in a sport? Do you ride your bike? Climb trees? Play tearing-around games with your friends? If not, try to do at least one of those things every day.

• Sometimes nervous energy can make a person want to jump out of her skin. So if you tend to keep your problems bottled up, talk to your parents or some other adult you trust about the things that are bothering you. Ask for ways to solve the problems so they aren't bugging you out of your chair all day.

• Channel your energy into the work you're doing at your seat. If you're reading, imagine what you're reading about, and pretend you're there. If you're writing, write as fast and as furiously as you can (within reason, of course!). If you're supposed to be putting your head down on your desk and resting (what silly teacher assigned *that*?), let your imagination run wild.

- Ask your teacher if you can have classroom chores to do when you finish your work, like straightening books, erasing the board, running errands. If you have to be up walking around, you might as well be useful!

- If having to sit still is such a problem for you that you can't concentrate on your work for more than a few minutes and you're feeling anxious and restless all the time, talk to your parents about that. There are a lot of physical reasons for feeling that way that need to be explored—and there are a lot of things adults can do to help you. (But just telling you to "Sit still!" isn't one of them!)

❀ *SUZY: I would like school if I had a different teacher.*

That's a tough problem. For one thing, the teacher is the person in authority, so you don't have a whole lot of options. For another, not every person gets along with every other person in the world (have you noticed?), even teachers. You might not like your teacher even if that person wasn't a teacher, but was instead the clerk at the grocery store or the lady who cuts your hair. What you can learn from being in a classroom with a teacher you don't care for is how to get along with difficult people—because your life is going to be full of them! Here are some thoughts to get you started:

- Make a private list of all the things you don't like about your teacher. Be specific. Just writing down, "She's mean" isn't going to help you much. "She yells too much" and "She acts like boys are better than girls" will. Be sure you keep this list completely to yourself. Write it in code if you have to!

- Go through your list and put a star by the three worst things ("She says 'shut up' to the class," "She tells me I'm not trying when I am," "She laughs at kids when they make a mistake.")

- Look at the things you didn't star. If your teacher got rid of those three things you think are the worst, could you deal with the things that don't have stars? Cross out the un-starred ones that wouldn't be so bad if she stopped doing the starred things.

- Now you have a shorter list. Pick the worst of the three starred things and decide what you could do to make that not so bad for yourself. If the teacher says "Shut up," to the class, try thinking about whether *you* have ever said it and how you felt at the time. You might actually "shut up" before she has to say it next time! Once you've worked on the first one, try the second one, and so on down the list. This does not ignore the fact that sometimes teachers do some pretty lousy things. And it doesn't mean you are responsible for every lousy thing they do! It does mean that if you can't change something, you can learn how to deal with it in a healthy way.

- If a teacher is being so mean that kids are crying in class or you don't think you can even ask for her help without being humiliated, by all means, talk to another adult about it. Start with your parents. It's up to them to go to the principal or some other authority and discuss the problem. Just be very sure you have your facts straight. No fair "busting" the teacher just because she won't let you pass notes to your girlfriends.

- Make a list of the teacher's good points. He or she is bound to have one or two! If he wears funny ties, doesn't give a ton of homework, and takes the class on field trips, tell him you like those things. Enjoy those parts to the fullest. Remember that a positive 'tude makes just about everything more bearable.

Talking to God About It

Dear ___Jesus___ *, (your favorite way of addressing God)*
I really want to have integrity when it comes to school so I can be the best me in the classroom, on the playground, in the cafeteria—well, you get the idea. There are some things I've read about in this chapter that really "hit home" with me. Would you please help me with the ones I've checked off here?

_____ *having a better attitude about school in general*
✓ *not being so bored in* ~~school~~ latin!
✓ *staying out of trouble in school*
_____ *making the most of the things I do like about school*
✓ *making the best of the things I don't like about school*
_____ *finding my niche in school*
✓ *getting over being anxious about tests and oral reports*
✓ *getting myself more organized*
✓ *getting help with work that's hard*
_____ *getting along with my teacher(s)*

And, God, thanks for the gift of a good education and for the things I do like about school, like:

___lots of friends + some cool teachers___

Please forgive me for my attitude problems, and help me to be forgiving of the things other people, even teachers, do in school to hurt my feelings or lead me into trouble, especially:

___Jack___

You're the best teacher, God, so please don't let me forget to come to you for everything when it comes to my education. I know you won't let me down.
I love you!

Katie ♡

A perfect day in school would be like this ...

fairly early, not tired.
Prakrit is right there. go to 1st
period together. Jack is not
annoying, stephen is also be ing funny.
Mr. Cardosi is in a good mood. PE=
DODGEBALL! Art= lots of fun!, Adam
isn't there. Math= Get all homework
done in class + we play: "Guess favorite #"
Lunch = PIZZA + ICE cream! Bio = Awsome!
& Adam! History = review
Game! Music = Recorders
+ I have a turn.
Go home w/
& HW.

Integrity Is Not a Spectator Sport

**Let us run with perseverance the race
marked out for us.**
Hebrews 12:1

ATTENTION ALL GIRLZ
DO NOT SKIP THIS CHAPTER
EVEN IF YOU AREN'T INTO SPORTS!!!!!

We're not going to be talking about how to be the best at kicking a soccer ball or the best at performing at the skating rink. We're going to talk about how to be the best *you* anytime you compete or watch other people compete.

This chapter is for girls like **Lily** who don't like to participate in *any* activity if they can't be the *best* at it—everything from spelling bees to the family "Who Can Have the Most Cavity-Free Visits to the Dentist" contest.

It's for girls like **Reni** who get so focused on winning at one thing that they practically ignore the rest of the world.

It's written especially for girls like **Suzy** who are kind, mild-mannered people everywhere except on the playing field, where they transform into bun-kicking little monsters.

It's a must for girls like **Zooey** who hate competition of any kind—not just sports but board games, costume contests, and guessing games on car trips!

And it's here for girls like **Kresha** who would love to compete in something—maybe a swimming race or a drawing contest—but are afraid they just aren't good enough, so they don't even try.

Not everybody is going to win—or even *dream* of winning—an Olympic gold medal, but everybody at some time in her life *is* going to be in a situation where she has to put her skills up against someone else's and see how she does. Sports are the first thing we think of, but they aren't the only activities that put you in competition mode. Ever participate in any of these?

- trying out for a play
- playing a game for prizes at a party
- trying to be top seller in a school fund-raiser
- playing Bible facts games for prizes or stickers in Sunday school
- entering reading contests
- challenging yourself to get the highest grade (or even just to pass!)
- seeing who among your friends can do anything the most or the longest— like jumping rope without missing, holding your breath under water, not talking, or not smiling!

- entering a talent competition
- entering a costume contest
- joining your cabin mates at having the cleanest cabin at summer camp

A complete list could fill up this whole book and more, but you get the idea. You can hardly get through a day without being involved in *some* kind of competition, because we human beings are a competitive bunch. We come out in the delivery room seeing if we can scream louder than any other baby who's ever been born!

Sometimes competition can be healthy—and sometimes it can bring out your fangs. So let's start with finding out when competition is a God thing, and when it isn't.

HOW IS THIS A God Thing?
God Wants You to Think: Win-Win

Everybody likes to win, and that's okay with God. What God *doesn't* like is when winning becomes more important than the basic things we always have to practice as Christians—loving God more than anything and loving others as much we love ourselves. Jesus said, "All the Law and the Prophets hang on these two commandments" (Matthew 22:40). So the following conditions for competing would hang nicely on those "pegs."

- The person you're competing with is as good as you are at what you're doing. Even the person who loses the competition will then win just by having the experience of competing with an equal. (What's the fun of beating a beginner at tennis if you've been playing for five years!)
- The competition isn't personal. You're not out to win because you despise your opponent or you think she's a snob and deserves to lose or because she beat you last time and you couldn't stand it—see what we mean?
- You can figure out a way to make everyone involved feel like a winner. For example, can you keep the competition friendly or plan a party for everybody afterwards to celebrate a great contest?
- You won't feel like your life is over if you lose.
- Even if you lose, you'll be glad you competed.

Balance Comfort and Courage

Competition can be a good thing when it helps you develop courage. It takes a lot of "guts" to try out for a play or play goalie in a big soccer game. And you'll know how to use those same "guts"—that same courage—later, when you have to compete for a job or fight for something you believe in. It's part of becoming a woman of integrity.

But competition can also work against you when you want to win so badly you'll risk something that you shouldn't—like losing a friend or possibly getting hurt. In one of his stories, Jesus told us we should always figure out what it's going to cost us to compete. "Suppose a king is about to go to war against another king," he said. "Will he not first sit down and consider whether he is able with ten thousand men to oppose the one coming against him with twenty thousand?" (Luke 14:31)

You need to do the same thing every time winning becomes important to you. Is what you're going to have to do, in order to win, worth the cost? What if you have to cheat to win? What if you have to play dirty by stretching the rules? What if you won't get the part if you don't make the other girl look bad? What if you have to neglect your schoolwork to get ready for the contest? That isn't courageous. It's just foolish.

Competition is also not such a good thing if the thought of losing is so scary to you, you don't even try to win—you don't even participate in the first place! Remember the story in the Gospel of Luke where Jesus tells about the guy who was asked to take care of some money? Unlike his friends who invested theirs, he hid it because he was so afraid of losing it (Luke 19:11–26). If there is no *real* danger—you're just afraid of losing—ask God to help you take the risk. As Jesus says, "to everyone who has, more will be given" (Luke 19:26). That doesn't mean you'll always win the game or the contest, but you *will* come out a braver and stronger person. And that's the whole reason for competition in the first place.

Think Team

A lot of the competition you're involved in is probably between teams or groups. When that's the case, it's important to remember that it isn't about you being the star or the hero. It's about what's good for your team and what's going to make everyone on it a winner, even if you don't go home on the bus with a trophy.

Jesus talked about that. When he told his disciples that he was going to be put to death but he would be raised up again, the mother of two of his followers asked Jesus to promise that her sons would have the highest places of honor in his kingdom. The other disciples were pretty disgusted about that and started griping to each other. So Jesus sat them down and told them it wasn't going to be that way with them or those who chose to follow him. He told them that anyone who wanted to be great must first be a servant—no trying to be first or best on his team. Everybody had to be in it together (Matthew 20:20–28). The same goes for you. Be a servant to your team.

Always Win by Getting Up Every Time You Fall Down

It doesn't take a rocket scientist to figure out that in most competitions, somebody wins and somebody loses. But losing a match, a game, or an election doesn't make you a loser. You can *always* be a winner if you don't let a loss keep you from trying again.

Jesus told a story about a widow who kept going to a judge and complaining because she wasn't winning in court—her rights were still being violated. After she nagged and whined and pleaded and badgered over and over, day after day, the judge finally saw to it that justice was done for her (Luke 18:1–5). The lesson in the story, of course, is that if we keep trying (that's called persistence) and asking for God's help, things will turn out according to his will. Whether you actually win or not, you are never a loser if you persist. It's integrity that makes you a winner.

Girlz WANT TO KNOW

Let's see what all that looks like when you actually find yourself in the middle of competition. The Girlz wanted to know too.

✿ *LILY: When I go to my brother's high school football games, I get so angry when the other team doesn't play fair or the referee makes a bad call or our team plays lousy, I want to smack somebody. Is that bad?*

It's one thing to get up there in the bleachers and really cheer your team on. That's part of the fun of sports, especially for people who don't actually play but still want to be involved. But as you've already figured out, sometimes that feels good and at other times you question whether you're doing something wrong (and "smacking somebody" would definitely fall into the category of doing something wrong). Good spectator sportsmanship requires integrity. Some examples will probably clear that right up for you.

SPECTATORS WITH INTEGRITY	SPECTATORS WITHOUT INTEGRITY
Just feel disappointed when the other team scores.	Boo the other team.
Yell up-beat cheers for their own team.	Yell cheers that put down the other team
Complain to their fellow fans when a referee makes a bad call.	Yell ugly stuff at the referee.
Feel concern when a player on the other team gets hurt.	Cheer when a player on the other team gets hurt.
Tell the fans for the other side that their team played a good game, even though they lost.	Laugh at the other fans when their team loses.
Ignore the other side's fans who try to pick a fight.	Say, "Bring it on!"

Resist the urge to get angry at the other team's fans because of stuff that's going on down on the field.	Take out their anger about what's going on down on the field with other teams fans.
Remember that it's just a game.	Cry and throw things when their team loses.
Support the players next time they see them, even if they lost.	Criticize the players for losing next time they see them.
Keep going to games, even when their team's not having a good season.	Stop going to games because they don't like to be grouped with "losers."

❀ *SUZY: My father turns everything in our house into a competition. I mean, seriously—everything. He has contests for who can bring home the best report card, who can get her chores done fastest, who goes the longest without getting grounded. My sisters really get into it, but I hate it. Is there any way I can get out of that?*

You obviously aren't a person who thrives on competition, at least not every minute of the day. It's okay to be that way—and if you lose a lot of those family contests, that doesn't mean you aren't as good a person as your sisters. On the other hand, your dad is probably just trying to prepare you girls for the adult world where there is definitely a lot of competition, and he's also trying to make you better and better at everything you do. Think about a few of the following approaches that might help you get the benefits of dad's contests without making yourself miserable in the process:

- Don't worry about winning or losing, unless of course, you get punished when you lose. Do your own personal best, and congratulate your sisters when they win. That way you don't go against your father's authority, but you're still true to yourself.
- Try to make the "contests" fun for yourself. Sing or listen to music on headphones while you rake leaves. Pretend you're Cinderella while you're doing chores.
- Make a big deal out of it when one of your sisters wins one of your dad's more important contests, like the report card competition. If your older sister gets straight A's and you make a B, write her a note on cute notepaper or bring her breakfast in bed. That way, you keep the whole thing from being cutthroat, and you learn good sportsmanship at the same time.

✿ *RENI: I'm first chair violin in my school orchestra, which means the director thinks I'm the best player in the violin section. I like being in that position, only now I'm always looking around, making sure nobody's getting good enough to challenge me. I really like some of the other violinists, so I feel kind of bad thinking that way.*

That's one of the problems lurking beneath the surface of healthy competition and waiting for a chance to turn it into something mean or fearful. You're already on the right track by realizing what you're doing and what it's doing to you. See if these suggestions help:

- Try to do your best and always let your best get a little better. Then leave it at that. If someone creeps up and steals first chair from you, you can honestly say you did all you could.
- Go out of your way to be nice and friendly to those people whose progress "threatens" you. Pray for them too. It's hard to be cutthroat with people when you pray for them and consider them your friends.
- Do what you can to keep reminding yourself that an orchestra—or any group or team—is not about any one person, not even the "number one"

player in the violin section. Help other players who are having trouble. Listen to the way other people play, even the cellos and the basses. Make up an orchestra cheer or slogan you can all do before or after practices.

✓ CHECK Yourself OUT & Just Do It

Now let's see how all that can work for you. Below you'll find one activity for each of the four things God says you need to practice when it comes to competition. Try to do all four—but don't try to do them all in one day!

1 Think Win-Win

On this line, write down one thing you're competing for right now. It can be anything in which you hope to do better than someone else. (Anything from trying to get picked for a team to trying to get more front seat privileges than your brother.) _____

Now check off all the things that are true about that competition on this list. Be *really* honest with yourself!

_____ 1. I don't care if I win—I just don't want to lose!

_____ 2. I'd be happy if the person I'm competing with made a mistake.

_____ 3. The person I'm competing with is equal to me.

_____ 4. The competition is about sports or school.

_____ 5. The competition is over a friend.

_____ 6. It involves getting even with somebody.

_____ 7. I don't care how good I am as long as I win.

_____ 8. It's not going to mean anything to me unless I win.

_____ 9. It's been going on a long time.

_____ 10. Winning this is going to get me something I've wanted for a long time.

_____ 11. Somebody else might be hurt somehow if I win.

_____ 12. I don't really care about winning—I just don't want the other person to win.

_____ 13. I might let the other person win because I hate conflict.

_____ 14. If I lose, I'm going to make winning miserable for the other person.

_____ 15. I think somehow everybody can be a winner in this.

_____ 16. If the other person wins, I'll celebrate with her.

_____ 17. I think maybe we can compromise.

_____ 18. If I lose, it isn't going to feel like the end of the world.

_____ 19. Being in this competition is going to make me better at what we're competing in.

_____ 20. Being in this competition is all I can think about.

If you put checks next to the following numbers, you're thinking win-win, and God probably smiles on your competition: 3, 4, 15, 16, 17, 18, 19.

These should always be your guidelines for competing in anything. If all seven of these are true in any situation, then you go, girl! If not, really think about the ones that are missing. Can you get those in there, or should you just say "No, thanks," to this competition?

If you put checks next to any of the other numbers, look at each one carefully. If it's obvious right away why that reason isn't a God thing, you'll know what to do. If not, go back and read the **How Is This a God Thing?** section.

✌ Balance Courage and Comfort

On the line below, write down one thing you're afraid to try right now. Maybe you're afraid because you might not be any good at it, or that you might lose, or that people might laugh at you—and yet you *really* want to give it a go. It can be anything from getting out on the skating rink when you've only skated in your own driveway to entering the grocery store coloring contest.

_____

In the **Comfort Column** write down all the reasons you're afraid. Don't think you're going to look like a wimp—nobody's going to read this but you! Don't do anything in the **Courage Column** yet.

Comfort Column   Courage Column

Now look at the items in your **Comfort Column**. Remember that these are the things that are keeping you comfortable. Sometimes they're good things— they protect you from harm. But sometimes they just keep you from taking good, healthy risks that might make your life more fun or more exciting or even more full of wisdom. So—circle any fear in the **Comfort Column** that you think you can conquer right now—stuff that no longer seems like a big deal. Write that in the **Courage Column**, even if it's only one thing. Here's Zooey's example.

"I want to try out for cheerleader, but I'm afraid because—

Comfort Column   Courage Column

Ashley and her friends are going to laugh at me, because only the really popular kids try out.

I've been practicing a lot and I'm pretty good, but I might get really nervous at the tryouts and blow it. People will say that I think I'm all that because I'm trying out.

Now you can focus on that one thing you're going to try to be more courageous about. Here are some suggestions:

- Pray about it. Not only does God want to know what's going on with you, but he can help you.
- Ask an adult friend to help you with your fear. It's always good to have guidance.

- Tell your very best friend what you're trying to do and ask her to let you know if she sees you slipping.
- Write your fear on a card and carry it in your pocket or your school bag. It'll be a reminder that you don't have to be a slave to that fear anymore.
- Write about your fear in your journal.
- Draw a cartoon showing you being held captive by your fear. Make the fear a silly monster who really has no power over you. Make it funny. Then draw one that shows you escaping.
- Treat yourself when you actually try that thing you're afraid of. Use some allowance to buy the Beanie Baby you've been wanting, or reread your favorite book for the fifteenth time. Fears can be hard to conquer so reward yourself!
- Don't forget to thank God for your victory.

Think Team!

Think about something that you're competing in that involves a group of people. It *can* be a sports team you're on, but it could also be something like your class trying to win a field trip by selling candy bars. Write it here:

_____

Remember that when you're competing *with* a group for something the whole group wants (not *against* the other people *in* the group), it can't be all about you. It has to be about all of you working together for a common goal. So—being completely honest (as always!)—put a star next to everything *you* are doing and thinking when you're working with that group:

_____   1. I try to get the team to do things my way.

_____   2. I always let other people have their own way on the team.

_____ 3. I let other people have some of what they want if I get to have some of what I want.

_____ 4. I try to get us to come up with the best possible way.

_____ 5. I think it's cool that some people in the group are different from most of us.

_____ 6. I put up with the fact that some people in the group are different from most of us.

_____ 7. I love it when things work out for the whole group.

_____ 8. I'm pretty much the star of my group.

_____ 9. I think everybody in the group has something to contribute.

_____ 10. I think some people in the group are more important than other people.

_____ 11. I wish everybody in the group was as creative as I am or worked as hard as I do.

_____ 12. When I think about it, everybody in the group has a different job.

_____ 13. I like the group the way it is, and I'm afraid if somebody else joined us they'd mess it up.

_____ 14. I don't want our group to become a clique.

_____ 15. I try to understand how other people in the group feel.

_____ 16. I try to help the other people in the group understand how I feel.

_____ 17. I'm kind of wishing I wasn't in this group because I do better on my own.

_____ 18. I'm proud to be part of this group.

If you put stars by these numbers, you have this being-a-member-of-a-group thing down pat: 4, 5, 7, 9, 12, 14, 15, 16, 18.

If you didn't put stars by *all* of those numbers, go back and look at the ones that don't have stars. This doesn't mean you are a lousy team member! It's just a way for you to find out where you might need to change your thinking.

Here are some suggestions for being a team or group member who competes with integrity:

- Give each person in your group an appreciation gift. Before you panic and run for your piggy bank, remember that appreciation doesn't have to cost money. Make each person a homemade card or ask your mom if you can bake a batch of those slice-the-dough cookies or pick a tiny bouquet of wildflowers for each person.

- Make a list of the people in your group. Beside each name, write down what that person brings to the group—anything from great ideas to great smiles.
- Suggest that the group celebrate a "hidden victory" together. We're not talking about winning a game or taking the school contest by storm, but a little "win" that has occurred along the way—like the fact that there hasn't been an argument in the group for a week. Get everybody to bring snacks. Put up a banner. Drink toasts to that mini-victory.
- Try to think of someone who might like to join your group. Check it out with the team and coach or with the group and its advisor, and then as a group, make a big ol' fun invitation—perhaps with balloons involved!

Or, hey, you could do invitations for a whole bunch of people. Or, if it's appropriate, even put up an open invitation in your school or church to *anybody* who wants to join in.

• If there's someone in your group who is somehow "different" from most of the other members—maybe by race or personality or a handicap—make a special effort to get to know that person. Invite her over to your house for a snack. Sit by her at the next meeting or practice. Think of a good question to ask her or a compliment you'd like to give her that you really mean.

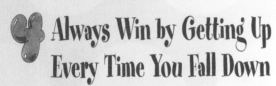

Always Win by Getting Up Every Time You Fall Down

Remember that winning doesn't mean you get the highest score or the biggest prize. It means never quitting, always picking yourself up when you feel defeated, learning from your mistakes, and turning your weaknesses into strengths.

Think about the last time you "lost" and write it here. It can be anything from not getting picked to play pitcher on your softball team, to not getting as many compliments from your mom for cleaning your room as your sister did.

_____

What did you do when you lost? Some examples might help:

_____

LILY: I stormed to my room and slammed the door when I got the call that my science project came in third.

RENI: I said the teacher was playing favorites when she didn't pick me for the solo.

ZOOEY: I quit the scrapbooking class when the teacher didn't choose my scrapbook for display.

SUZY: I cried when our team lost the city championship.

KRESHA: I wished the girl that got the award for Best ESL Student would fall on her face in front of everybody when she went up to get her certificate.

You: _____

    Now see if you can figure out what your next step, as a *real* winner, might be. Read the examples before you try to come up with one for your "loss."

LILY: I could look at the second and first place projects and see how I could make mine even better next year than it was this year.

RENI: I could ask the teacher how I could improve my playing so I could be solo material in the future.

ZOOEY: I could go back to the scrapbooking class and this time do it for the fun of it because, for Pete's sake, it's crafts—not World War III!

SUZY: I could ask my mom if we could have a cookout at our house for the team so we could celebrate that we got all the way to the finals.

KRESHA: I could put a note that says this—in English!—in my locker: "When you're learning a new language, your only competition is your-self. Just do your best."

You: _____

Talking to God About It

Dear _____ *(your favorite way of addressing God)*

Whew! I never knew I competed so much—no wonder these things happen to me a lot:

_____ I get angry.

_____ I get frustrated.

_____ I get really tired.

_____ I don't have as much fun playing games and participating in sports as I used to.

_____ I argue a lot.

_____ I think I'm a loser.

God, would you please help me with the ones I've checked off? And would you please help me with these areas that really get me into competition-trouble?

And most of all, God, would you puh-leeze help me remember that when all is said and done, the only victory I really have to win is the victory over the rottenness that exists in the world—and that as long as I keep turning to you, I've already won?

Thanks, God, for making me a winner. You're the world's best coach.

is a REAL winner, and here's why ...

_____
_____
_____
_____
_____
_____
_____
_____
_____
_____
_____
_____
_____

Join the Integrity Club

The integrity of the upright guides them.
Proverbs 11:3

When the final bell rings at school, the Girlz grab their backpacks and coats and other assorted "stuff" and head for the door. School's out—and it's the best time of the day! Or at least, that's what they've been told it *should* be. But—

When it comes to extracurricular activities—you know, the after-school clubs and organizations—**Lily** has so much going on, she usually has to stop and think which thing she's supposed to do that day. Is it Drama Club, student government, or school newspaper? And is this the one where she's president, secretary, or committee chairperson? Yikes!

Kresha dutifully follows Lily to Drama Club or Suzy to French Club. She would secretly rather be going to Chess Club, but none of the other Girlz belongs to it, and wouldn't it be scary to go to a group none of her friends goes to?

Reni grabs her violin case and heads for the music suite. She'd actually like to be in that "environmental group" that's starting up, where they're going to recycle stuff and campaign against pollution, but there's no way. Orchestra takes up every free minute she has.

Zooey just watches her four friends and wishes she could be like them—always wrapped up in doing cool things. If only she knew what she wanted to do!

The Girlz all know that after-school activities are important, and you probably do too. They give you a lot of things the regular old school day can't—things like:

- a chance to really get to know people who like the same kinds of things you do. There's never enough time for that when you're taking spelling tests and working on those wretched math problems.
- time to explore those things that attract your attention, the way science projects and grammar drills might not. While you barely get to read one paragraph out loud in class, you can spend a whole *hour* reading one scene over and over in Drama Club!
- fun! Let's face it—although a lot of teachers try to make schoolwork enjoyable, things like memorizing the states and capitols are usually just plain work. But the things you do in your club meetings—like make

quiche in French Club or go on a field trip to a gallery with the Art Club—are nothing but fun!

- the kind of learning you don't have to stress out over. It matters if you flub up a social studies test, but if you trip over your own boots on an Adventure Club hike, it's not gonna go on your report card.
- a part of your education you won't get in the class-room. It's important for all of us to have reading, writing, and math skills, and that takes up just about all the classroom time you have for twelve years. But there's *so* much more to know. You really have to use the whole world as your schoolroom, and being in organized after-school activities teaches you how to do that. You won't belong to the Spanish Club forever, but being a member now can teach you how to appreciate the food and music and traditions of another culture so that as you get older you can explore French and Egyptian and Venezuelan cultures on your own.

But as the Girlz have found out, those same wonderful extracurricular activities carry their own hidden dangers:

- You can take on too many of them and wind up not enjoying any.
- You can participate in things that aren't right for you, sometimes just because your friends are in them, and *not* join in on those things that really *are* your thing just because everybody else considers them uncool.
- You can just be too afraid to try anything, because you think you'll stink at it or nobody who's in it will like you.
- You can take it way too seriously and miss out on the fun of being a kid.

So what do you do to make sure you get into the *right* activities and the right *number* of activities and have the right *attitude* toward those activities— without freaking out in the process? Naturally—you see what God has to say about it.

HOW IS THIS A God Thing?

No—they didn't call them extracurricular activities in biblical times, and as far as we know there was no Drama Club, no school newspaper, no cheerleading squad, no concert band (unless you want to count David and his harp). But people who had interests in common did group together, and God showed them the right way to do it—the way that showed integrity.

God's Step One: "The fear of the LORD [respect for] is the beginning of knowledge" (Proverbs 1:7). We've already said that after-school activities are part of your education, so when you're deciding which club to join, think and pray about what God wants you to do. You might be thinking, "Oh, come on! God has more important things to think about than what I'm gonna do between three and five in the afternoon"—but you're wrong! God wants to be part of every decision you make. Besides, "fools despise wisdom and discipline" (Proverbs 1:7). You definitely don't want to be a "fool"—it's right up there with "geek." You say you don't know how to consult God on issues like this? We'll get to that in **Just Do It**, so stand by.

God's Step Two: "Walk in the ways of good men and keep to the paths of the righteous" (Proverbs 2:20). Only take part in those activities that the "good kids" join. You may love computers, but if all the other people in the Computer Club are into hacking into the principal's private files or exploring yucky stuff on the Internet, it would be a good idea to make another choice. On the other hand, your current friends are probably not the only kids who are "good." Try not to shy away from a club you'd like to look into just because you don't know anybody in it. Shared interests have a way of bonding people very quickly.

God's Step Three: "The LORD protects the simplehearted" (Psalm 116:6). As you choose your activities, remember that being involved in things is not about showing off and getting your name on every page of the school yearbook. It's about living a full life, one that is simply filled with the things that make your mind happy, that make you want to jump out of bed in the morning. A person with integrity isn't running to get into the "Look at all the things I can do!" spotlight.

God's Step Four: "It is a trap for a man to dedicate something rashly and only later to consider his vows" (Proverbs 20:25). Be very sure you've chosen a club that's right for you before you make promises to it, because a person with integrity *keeps* her promises. That includes the vow you make to your parents that you aren't going to quit right after they fork over fifteen bucks for the club T-shirt! We all make errors in judgment, so to avoid that, give yourself time to get to know the people in a group and understand all that's expected of the members before you raise your hand and say, "I'm in!"

God's Step Five: "The plans of the diligent lead to profit" (Proverbs 21:5). As you're choosing extracurricular activities, look at your *whole* schedule and make sure you have time for all the clubs you're committing to. It might not seem like too much to have Drama Club on Mondays and school yearbook on Tuesdays and Thursdays, but when you add in your church group on Wednesday nights and city league soccer on Wednesday and Friday afternoons, and then realize there will be rehearsals every afternoon for the Drama Club play when it goes into production—and then remind yourself that you're also going to have homework and chores.... You get the picture. A good rule of thumb is to leave yourself at least two afternoons a week with nothing scheduled. Otherwise, none of the things you do will "lead to profit."

God's Step Six: "A simple man believes anything, but a prudent man gives thought to his steps" (Proverbs 14:15). Always run your plans by your parents before you promise to join anything. Yeah, you're becoming more independent as you learn to make good decisions, but your mom and dad are still the best at knowing how much time and energy you have for extracurricular stuff. You might not like some of the choices they make, but give them a chance. Most of the time, you'll see they were right. (Don't you hate it when that happens?)

CHECK
Yourself OUT

Let's see where you stand on the steps that lead to choosing the right activities. In each situation described below, choose the option that sounds *most* like where you are right now (being as honest as you can be, of course). Then, read what your choices may tell you about your extracurricular self.

1. When I pray about joining a club or activity:

   a. I ask God to guide me and then I wait for a peace that tells me the answer.

   b. I join first and then ask God to bless what I've chosen to do.

   c. Oh . . . am I supposed to pray about stuff like that?

2. When it comes to the other people in any group I'm thinking of joining:

   a. I check them out carefully, and I don't join if most of them don't seem to have the kind of integrity we've been talking about in this book.

   b. I figure I'm okay with anybody as long as *I* have *my* stuff together when it comes to God.

   c. I don't think it makes any difference, so I don't actually check them out at all.

3. I usually join a club or a group or an activity because:

   a. it's something I really enjoy or want to learn about.

   b. everybody else is joining it.

c. being involved in a lot of activities helps you be popular.

4. When I join a club or group:

   a. I find out what all the requirements are first.

   b. I am sometimes surprised by what's expected of me once I get into it.

   c. I figure if it gets to be too much for me, I can always quit.

5. The number of after-school activities I'm involved in:

a. leaves me enough time for homework, chores, and just hanging out.

b. leaves me just enough time for homework and chores.

c. means I have to juggle things around a lot and sometimes not get to my homework and chores.

6. When it comes to my extracurricular activities, I ask my parents:

   a. to help me make sure I'm picking the right ones and have enough time to give them each my best.

   b. to help me out when things get tangled up or too stressful.

   c. to leave me alone and let me handle it myself—except for transportation and money, of course.

So what do your answers mean?

Any **c** answer *may* mean you're flying into things before you consider:

- what God wants you to do.
- whether the members are kids you want to spend time with.
- whether your reasons for joining are good ones.
- whether you can do all the things that are going to be expected of you.
- whether you really have the time to give it your very best.
- what your parents have to say about it.

As you read on, you'll learn how to check out those problem areas, so that your life isn't so stressed and tangled and rushed all the time. Nowhere in the Bible does it say God wants us to run around like headless chickens!

Any **b** answer *could* mean that you consider those six things (in the list above)—but maybe not *before* you sign on the dotted line! If you find yourself saying, "Oops," or "I'm gonna have to quit," or "I'm sorry, but I can't—" read on. You'll learn how to consider those helpful guidelines *before* you get yourself into an "oops" situation.

Any **a** answer *probably* means you're headed in the right direction in that area—but read on. It never hurts to have a little refresher course in the ways of integrity. You already have the knack for keeping things balanced and peaceful and fun—so why not get even better at it?

Girlz WANT TO KNOW

There are a few more bugaboos you could run into when it comes to your out-of-the-classroom learning activities. Our Girlz have experienced them, so hopefully our answers for them can help you too.

✿ *LILY: It seems like every group I get into, I get picked to be the leader. I kind of like that, but sometimes it gets me into problems. Are there any rules for being the leader?*

As a matter of fact, there *are* some guidelines, and wouldn't you know they'd come right from the Bible? (There's nothing that book can't help you with!) Here are a few that might help you now, even when you're no older than twelve:

- "Make plans by seeking advice" (Proverbs 20:18). Basically, that means choose an adult who knows something about your group and ask that person to be your advisor all along the way. Don't try to do it all alone—and we don't just say that because you're a kid. The President of the United States has a whole staff of advisors to help him run the country!
- If you're the president of a club, ask if you can meet with your club advisor at least every other week. If you're in charge of a committee, sit down

with the grown-up in charge and make a list of all that person expects you and your committee to accomplish, and don't be afraid to go back to that adult whenever you have a question or run into a problem.

- "The king's heart is in the hand of the LORD; he directs it like a water-course wherever he pleases" (Proverbs 21:1). Everyday that you are the leader, director, or chairman of a group, ask God to help you do what he'd like to see done. He pretty much spells that out in Matthew, Mark, Luke, and John whenever Jesus talks about getting along with people. So have your parents or your youth pastor or your Sunday school teacher help you look for those passages. You could memorize them or write a few down to keep in your backpack as reminders. If you're doing the God thing, you can't go wrong as one of his leaders.

- Remember, "If a ruler listens to lies, all his officials become wicked" (Proverbs 29:12). One of the most important jobs of a leader is to make sure everything that happens in the group is honest and fair. It can really be hard when some group member runs to you and says, "Susie Schmo is saying you aren't a good president, and she's gonna do everything she can to make you quit." Do you believe that? Do you get upset and resign? Do you try to get back at Susie Schmo by spreading evil stuff about *her*? None of the above! You don't listen to talk like that, but go on doing the best job you can.

- "If a king judges the poor with fairness, his throne will always be secure (Proverbs 29:14). It's easy when you're the top dog to forget about those members who don't speak up very much and tend to get pushed around by the more outspoken kids. Make it a point to ask the quieter people what they think and what they'd like to see done. Put one of them in charge of a committee if she's willing. Those "Pick me! Pick me!" people might not like it at first, but they'll respect you when they see how much better the group works when *everybody* has a voice.

- Most important of all: "Love and faithfulness keep a king safe; through love his throne is made secure" (Proverbs 20:28). That pretty much says it all, doesn't it?

❀ *SUZY: Sometimes I think I could do a better job of leading a group than the kid that's running it, but I never get elected because I'm quiet. Do you have to be a loudmouth to be the leader?*

Not at all! And just because somebody is a loudmouth doesn't mean she's automatically going to make a good president or chairperson. The mark of a good leader is the ability to listen to what each of the members has to say, and it sounds like you would be good at that. But how do you get yourself elected when everyone else is shouting you down? Try these ways to give people the idea that you are ready to be promoted to a place of honor:

- Sit up front, close to the current leader, who is running the meeting. That way you can make eye contact.
- Be an active listener, nodding your head when you agree with what's being said, asking questions to clear things up.
- Volunteer for the next thing that comes up that you would like to help with. It doesn't have to be the chairmanship of a committee right away. Prove that you're a good worker, and people will remember that.
- Then tell the leader or the advisor, privately, that you would like to be in charge of a particular committee or job. If that doesn't happen right away, don't pout—just wait for the next opportunity to ask.
- If you're in a small group and somebody who's in charge falls behind, volunteer to pick up the slack.
- The next time an election comes up, talk to people in the group about your desire to have an office. By then, they'll know who you are and what kind of work you can do. Don't be surprised if you turn out to be the winner! If you don't, there's always next time. Don't go away mad. After all, it's the good of the group that's most important, right?

❀ *ZOOEY: What if none of the clubs at my school sound good to me? I've tried joining clubs just to be with Suzy or Lily, but I always end up dropping out because it's not my thing. But then I feel like a loser, you know?*

You have one very positive thing going for you, Zooey—you know that being involved in some kind of after-school activity is important. There are a lot of kids who would just as soon be couch potatoes—and that's not you. But the fact that you haven't found your niche yet doesn't make you a loser. We have two suggestions that might help chase that feeling away:

- Make a list of all the things you *do* like to do for fun. It might include things like baking cookies, taking pictures, going clothes shopping, and making scrapbooks. It's okay if they aren't the typical activities schools have clubs for. Then, look at a list of the clubs and activities your school does offer and see if any of them have anything in common with the things you like to do. Maybe there's an art club. Photography is an art. So is designing cool scrapbook pages. You could learn tons of stuff in an art club that would make your picture-taking and scrapbook-making even more fun and cool.
- If there is absolutely *no* activity that has anything in common with your thing, consider starting one. Maybe you'd join a photography club if there were one, or a cooking group, or a learn-to-sew kind of thing so you could make your *own* cool clothes. Figure out which teacher on staff might be good at sponsoring a group like that and ask that person if he or she has time to be an advisor. If that doesn't work, try for a non-school get-together. Does that retired lady across the street help you with cookies? Would she be willing to meet with you and a couple of other would-be bakers once a week to try new recipes? Use your imagination and the wisdom of the adults around you—you'll be amazed at what can happen.

Just Do It

There are two sets of activities here. Choose the set that best fits you—or do both if you want. We guarantee you'll have extracurricular fun!

SET I. For those who aren't involved in extracurricular activities and would like to be or know they should be (or whose parents are telling them they *have* to be!).

Step 1. Get a list of the extracurricular activities your school offers. If you're home-schooled or your school doesn't provide those kinds of things, get a list of community offerings for kids from your local community center, YMCA, or your church (or *somebody's* church if you don't have one!). Have a grown-up help you get your hands on such a list if you don't know where to start.

Step 2. Before you look at the list, have a talk with God. Using the best prayer method for you (praying silently, praying out loud, writing prayers in your journal, drawing them, whatever), ask God to help you find at least one activity that will help you grow as a person and let you have some fun at the same time. Then pay attention. Watch for opportunities to come your way as you begin your search. Wait for a feeling of "this is right"

when you consider a choice. Those are the ways God answers such prayers.

Step 3. Study the list carefully, looking for an activity that fits these requirements:

a. It's something *you* are really interested in.

b. It's something you would join because you like that sort of thing, rather than because all the cool kids are in it or it would give you a chance to show off.

c. It's not something that would take up more time than you have to spare (Be especially careful about sports, performance groups, and competitive academic things like Olympics of the Mind. Those are great activities, but they're best for people who aren't involved in other things as well).

Step 4. Discuss it with your parents. Listen to what they have to say, because they may know things about this particular activity that you aren't aware of. For example, it may require you to have expensive equipment or it might conflict with the family's schedule (practices right at dinnertime, that kind of thing). You can try to work some of those things out, but be willing to be flexible or to accept a "Not this time."

Step 5. Give yourself at least one or two meetings with the group before you make a commitment to join. Look carefully at these two things:

a. The other kids in the group—are they friendly and do they seem to get along for the most part. If so, that's a good sign. Look for cliques or "taking sides," which are danger signs. And be sure the group isn't involved in something you don't want to be involved in, like excluding certain people or breaking rules.

b. The things you would be promising to do—club rules say you can't miss any meetings or you have to provide snacks once a month or you have to sing a solo before the end of the year and you can't do those things. Don't say you will and then make excuses later. After all, part of having integrity is keeping your promises.

Step 6. Once you've done all of that and you're as sure as you can be that this is the "thing" for you—go for it with all the integrity you can muster. You're going to have a blast and learn tons of good stuff.

SET II. For those who are already involved in at least one after-school activity.

Step 1. Under each weekday listed below, write the activities you're involved in after school hours on those days. Include sports, lessons, church stuff, and performance activities as well as school groups and clubs.

MONDAY	TUESDAY	WEDNESDAY	THURSDAY	FRIDAY

Step 2. Answer these questions about your activities. Look back at your "calendar" above as often as you need to:

a. Are any of these activities things you think God might not be so crazy about? Do any of them make you uneasy? Are there any that interfere with something you'd like to be doing at church? Do any of them wear you out so you barely have any quiet time with God? Put a small check mark next to any activity on your calendar that you had to give a "yes" answer for.

b. Are there any kids in those activities that do things you're not allowed to do (like use bad language, act disrespectfully to adults, put people down, that kind of thing)? Do you ever find yourself doing things with one of those groups that you wouldn't do on your own because you know it isn't really right? Put a small check mark next to any activity on your calendar you had to give a "yes" answer for (even if there's already a check mark there).

c. Are you in any of those activities *only* because:
  • the popular kids are in it, or all your friends are in it?
  • you've been in it a long time and you don't want to be a quitter?
  • you're afraid to tell your parents you want to quit?

Put a small check mark next to any activity on your calendar you had to give a "yes" answer for (even if there's already a check mark there).

d. Have you made promises to any group that you've found out you can't keep? Are you doing anything in any group or activity that you're only doing because it's required? Are you failing to keep a promise to any group for any reason at all? Put a small check mark next to any activity on your calendar you had to give a "yes" answer for (even if there's already a check mark there).

e. Do you ever have to miss a meeting or practice because it conflicts with another activity you're in? Do you ever have to stay up too late to finish homework because you're involved in an activity? Do you ever fail to do your homework or study for a test because you're so busy with an

82

after-school activity? Are you ever too tired or too busy to get your chores done because of lessons and practices and that kind of thing? Do you ever wish you could just go home and "veg out" instead of going to a meeting or a practice? You know the drill—put a small check mark next to any activity on your calendar for which you had to answer "yes" to any question.

f. Do your parents ever complain about any of your activities? Do your parents ever seem cranky when they pick you up or drop you off at an activity because they're tired from driving you around? Do you ever argue with your parents about things related to any of your extracurricular activities? One more time—put a small check mark next to any activity on your calendar for which you had to answer "yes" to any question.

Step 3. Study your calendar with its check marks now, and—

a. If there are five check marks next to any activity, get rid of that one right away—or at least consider it and talk it over with your mom or dad. It's apparently not a God thing because it doesn't provide good relationships for you, you're in it for the wrong reasons, you can't meet its requirements, you don't have time for it, and your parents don't like it. So why not get the heck out of it! Life is too short to be wasting time on something that's wrong for you in every way possible!

b. If there are three or four check marks next to any activity, study it very carefully. With that many strikes against it, it calls for a careful look at whether it's a God thing—whether the other kids in it are good friends for you right now, whether you're in it for the right reason, whether you can do all that's expected of you, whether you have time for it, and whether your parents are really happy with your involvement in it. No activity is absolutely perfect, but when there are three or four things that are *so* not-perfect, you might want to consider dropping it from your schedule, looking for another group that does the same thing, or waiting until some other activity is over. Your mom or dad or even the group's adult leader can help you make that decision. Remember that you're supposed to be having fun while you learn from something you enjoy. Anything else isn't the best use of your time.

c. If you had only one or two check marks next to an activity, look at it to see if that one problem or challenge can be solved without having to give up the activity or drop out of the group. Maybe the only thing wrong with it is that you are over scheduled and barely have time to breathe. Could you give it up for now and do it during the summer when you aren't in school or at a time when one of your other activities is over? Or perhaps the only issue is that your folks don't have the money for a cheerleading uniform or a set of watercolors. Could you put off being a cheerleader or joining the art club until you can save up enough money to pay for the things you'll need yourself? Of course, if the only real problem with a club is that all the people in it have taken a vow to have their belly buttons pierced, there's not much compromising you can do there! In a case like that, maybe you could start your own group, huh?

d. If you had no check marks, it looks like you're in pretty good shape activity-wise! If at any time you should feel uneasy about any of your after-school activities, though, run them through the questions you just asked yourself. It's easy to get into a rut or a tangle—and not so hard to get out or unsnarl once you know what the problem is.

e. If doing the above has left you with no activities—don't despair! Go back to **SET I** and go through those steps. There's something for everybody. Don't miss out on the fun!

Talking to God About It

Dear _____, *(your favorite way of addressing God)*

Thanks so much for making the world such a fun, learning-packed place to grow up. And thanks for letting me see that I have the challenges I've checked off below:

_____ *finding an activity I like*

_____ *making sure my activities are things you want for me*

_____ *finding the right people to be in groups with*

_____ *choosing activities for the right reasons*

_____ *keeping my promises to the groups and teams I join*

_____ *using my after-school time wisely*

_____ *listening to my parents when it comes to my extracurricular activities*

Would you please help me with those things? And would you please forgive me for the mistakes I've made in those areas in the past, especially when I _____.

Most of all, God, please help me to know when you're pleased with the choices I've made and the things I'm doing with my free time. Please help me to:

_____ *take time to talk to you everyday.*

_____ *take time to listen for you everyday.*

_____ *pay attention to feelings of peacefulness and uneasiness.*

_____ *read and understand your wisdom in the Bible.*

I know you're with me every step of the way. I love you for that.

If I could design the perfect club, it would be like this ...

_____
_____
_____
_____
_____
_____
_____
_____
_____
_____

Unbreakable Faith

Worship the Lord your God, and serve him only.
Matthew 4:10

Lily has been going to church ever since she was carried in sucking on a pacifier, and her family talks about God as naturally as they discuss baseball scores and phone privileges. She's learned how to talk to God to find out what God wants her to do, and her parents help her make decisions based on that. Lily really loves God—which is why the doubts she's been having lately about some God things are a little scary. Is she still a good Christian, she wonders, even though there are moments when she wonders if everything she's been taught is really true?

Reni has also been raised by Christian parents, and she can give you a Bible verse for just about any subject you can come up with. She and her family are in the church every time the doors open. But lately she's begun to feel restless. What about all those other religions? And, for that matter, does she need a "religion" at all? Can't she worship God on her own—and sleep in on Sunday mornings?

Suzy wasn't brought up in the church and has only recently started going. It's fun being part of it with her friends, and every time there's an opportunity to go forward and say she wants to "invite Jesus into her heart," she feels like it would make them happy if she got up and did it. But she's not sure exactly what "invite Jesus into her heart" means, and she's shy about asking. Should she just go ahead and do it, or stick around and hope somebody tells her sooner or later?

Zooey goes to church with the Girlz, too, because, after all, she's not one to like being left out of things. It's all right most of the time, but when the congregation really gets into the singing and people start waving their hands in the air, she gets embarrassed. Still, even though she doesn't get what they're all worked up about, if one of the Girlz does it, she joins in too. Who wants to look like an oddball?

Kresha, bless her heart—she's so in love with life that she embraces anything that seems wonderful. She loves to go to church with the Girlz and sing the praise songs and exchange the peace with people. But she would be just as excited about doing a Native American ceremonial dance, practicing a Jewish song, or burning incense in a Buddhist temple. Isn't it okay, she says, as long as she's worshiping *some* kind of god?

All the Girlz—and maybe you—have some integrity issues when it comes to church, just like you do with school or extracurricular activities. But it's a little different with church, because we think, "Shouldn't we just naturally have integrity about church stuff because we believe in God? Don't we exhibit integrity just by showing up?"

No, not automatically. That's certainly part of it. You show that you *want* to be whole (have integrity) by doing the church thing. But just because you're there every Sunday doesn't mean you have integrity in your spiritual life. That needs work just like your school integrity and your competition integrity. In fact, it probably needs *more* work—because it's the most important kind of integrity you can have. God even says so!

HOW IS THIS A God Thing?

Jesus was gentle and loving with most people—especially the ones who had really messed up their lives, like thieves, prostitutes, and tax collectors. He knew they'd made their mistakes because they didn't know God. But when it came to people like the Pharisees who were all *about* the church and never let anybody forget it, look out! Jesus went on the rampage!

And why? Because they were the very people who *should* have been the closest to God and who *should* have accepted the thieves and tax collectors in the same loving way he did—but they didn't.

What Jesus expected of them was integrity. If they were going to call themselves people of God, then they had to be whole and complete in every way God required of them or they at least had to be *trying* to be that way. And that wholeness—that integrity—had to be *real*. It couldn't just be a show.

"Be careful not to do your 'acts of righteousness' before men, to be seen by them," he told the people. "If you do, you will have no reward from your Father in heaven" (Matthew 6:1).

"When you pray, do not be like the hypocrites, for they love to pray standing in the synagogues and on the street corners to be seen by men," he went on. "I tell you the truth, they have received their reward in full" (Matthew 6:5).

That was the way he explained it to the people. To the Pharisees themselves, the supposed leaders, he let loose!

"Woe to you, teachers of the law and Pharisees, you hypocrites!" (Matthew 23:13).

And then he told them just exactly *why* he called them "hypocrites" (fakes, phonies):

- They would turn themselves inside out to convert somebody, and then they'd turn that person into someone just like themselves: all talk and no action.
- They made up stupid rules for when a promise was a real promise and when they could get away without keeping it (like crossing their fingers behind their backs).
- They kept careful accounts of their money, but they were totally careless about things like fairness and kindness.
- They got all hung up on appearances (beards just the right length, that kind of thing), but they were slobs on the inside (like letting poor people die in poverty).
- They led people to believe they were saints (never making a mistake), when inside they were far from it (had evil thoughts and were greedy).
- They built big, beautiful temples to God, but they murdered his prophets.

Then Jesus wound it up with this lovely string: "You snakes! You brood of vipers! (Matthew 23:33)

It's pretty clear how God *doesn't* want us to act when it comes to him! (Ya think?) But Jesus didn't leave it at that. He explained over and over what spiritual integrity *is*. One of the best explanations is in what we call "The Beatitudes" (Matthew 5:3–11).

Jesus said that you are whole and complete when:

- you stop trying to run the show and let God run it.
- you admit when you're lost and let God comfort you.
- you're content with just who God made you to be.
- you truly care about other people.
- you get your inside world—your mind and heart—put right, so you can see God around you.

- you show people how to cooperate instead of compete and fight.
- you speak up for God even when you know people are going to make fun of you.
- you put up with people calling you a Jesus freak or spreading rumors that you're some kind of religious weirdo.

We could sum it up in one command: *When it comes to God, be real.*

 CHECK Yourself OUT

Usually at this point, we would give a quiz so you could find out just how much integrity you have when it comes to your relationship with God—but since none of us is where we should be yet (because we're so human—go figure!), it would make more sense to figure out what would be the best way for you personally to get closer to God. The more *real* your relationship with God is, the more *real* you will be. So this very different kind of quiz works like this.

Imagine that someone you love very much is going away for a long time. Maybe you don't even know how long it will be before you see that person again. Of course, you want to stay connected to the person, but you know it's going to be hard because you won't be able to *see* your loved one. You're afraid you'll forget—afraid your friendship will fade. But you aren't going to just let it go—you want to try to keep your relationship strong even though you won't be seeing this person you love.

Below are four ways you could stay connected. Put a star (*) next to the one that appeals to you the most, the one you know you would actually *do*. It's okay to put a star next to more than one if you have trouble making a decision!

_____ a. You would write letters to that person—a *lot*! You'd tell everything that was happening, ask all kinds of questions, and probably decorate your envelopes with stickers and drawings. Of course there would be at least a half a page of X's and O's at the end for hugs and kisses.

_____ b. You would save all your allowance and birthday money and the change you found in the couch cushions to call the person long distance. Then you would talk and talk until you ran out of money and had to start saving all over again. While you were collecting funds, you would also be collecting all the little details you'd share during your next conversation.

_____ c. You would put together a scrapbook of things the two of you have shared—maybe ticket stubs from movies you saw together, pictures of both of you laughing hysterically, shells you collected side-by-side at the beach. You would always be adding more stuff to your scrapbook, asking your friend to send you additions to make more memories.

_____ d. You would take time every day to get very quiet and imagine yourself with this person you love so much. In your mind, you would picture the two of you together. You might even feel as if you were hearing your conversations. It would seem so real that it would be as if that person were right there with you.

Now shift your thinking a little bit. Instead of that loved one being a person, think of God—the one who deserves all the love you can give. Just like a living person you can't see, God wants you to stay in touch with him so you don't forget how much you mean to each other. The best way for you personally, in your own unique way, to keep connected with a human loved one is the *same* best way for you to hold God in your thoughts. Let's see how that works.

If you chose (a)—the letter-writing approach—you're a person who communicates best by putting your thoughts on paper. Think about it—don't you also like to pass notes to your friends (even when you could just as easily talk to them)? Write in a diary (even if you don't do it every day like you promised yourself you would)? Make lists of stuff to do or buy (whether you ever do or buy anything or not)? So writing to God might be your best way to communicate what you're feeling and thinking and hoping and dreading. Sound kind of funky? We'll explain in the **Just Do It!** section.

If choice (b) was the one you picked—the let's-have-a-chat method—you would much rather talk to someone than communicate in any other way. It's a no-brainer really. Don't you enjoy talking to your friends—or just about anybody else, for that matter—on the phone? Don't you just about explode between recesses in school because you want to tell your best friend something *really* important? Haven't you been told that you have "the gift of gab" (or that you're a motor mouth!)? Then it makes sense that talking right out loud would be your best way to tell God what's on your mind, what you need, what you're thankful for. "Yeah," you may be thinking, "but God doesn't exactly answer, so …" Not to worry—we'll explain in the **Just Do It!** section.

If you selected choice (c), you are a hands-on kind of person, and chances are you would rather *do* something for a faraway friend than write a letter or make a phone call. Look at it this way: don't you get a kick out of creating birthday cards, making Christmas presents, collecting your classmates' autographs, bringing home souvenirs to your friends when you go on a trip? Then why would you communicate with God any differently? If that boggles your mind, don't despair! We'll explain in the **Just Do It!** section.

Did you put a star by choice (d)? You're probably a person who doesn't always have to say or do something to communicate with the people you love. It's the way you hold them in your mind that draws you close to them. It's a pretty safe bet that when it comes to your friends, you can tell when they're feeling left out or disappointed before they even tell you, right? You always seem to know what will make them laugh, don't you? And if you have to tell a friend that she's hurt your feelings, you rehearse the conversation in your head first, huh? That's why just imagining God, sensing God's presence, almost hearing the two of you talking is your best way to stay close. How does that work? Stay tuned for the **Just Do It!** section.

Just Do It!

In this section, just as we promised, there are some *real* activities to help your relationship with God to be—well—more *real*—and that means, of course, to have more integrity. Remember two things before you dive in (and we hope you *will* dive in!):

1. No matter how you answered the **Check Yourself Out Quiz,** read about all four of the different kinds of activities and feel free to try any of them. The quiz was just a way of showing you that there is a way for *everyone* to get closer to God.
2. It isn't all up to you to have a close relationship with God. In fact, God does most of the work. It's God who makes you want to be intimate (close) in the first place. It's God who turns your thoughts toward the light and warmth and love that are God. It's God who responds to your reaching out with answers to your prayers and that wonderful peaceful feeling that assures you everything really *is* going to be all right. These activities are just to help you do *your* part—and God loves it when you do that.

For Choice (A) People-The Writers

- Write a short letter to God, if not every day then as often as you can. Write as you would to a friend that you love and respect. Go ahead and decorate your little "epistles." Collect them in a God Notebook that only you will read unless you really want to share it with someone.

- You can also—or instead—keep a diary, but instead of writing "Dear Diary," write "Dear God" (or however you like to address our Lord). Your Talking to God Diary or Journal can be a collection of little snippets and thoughts you want to share with God, or it can include long rambling strings of stuff, or it can consist of a list of things God has done for you and taught you. Anything goes.
- If you sometimes think in poems or songs, write those for God. You can keep them in a special God Box that you decorate and keep in a private place.
- Write down your questions for God and pray that God will answer them. Keep your questions in your God Notebook or your Talking to God Journal or your God Box and read them every now and then. You'll be amazed at how many of them have been answered while you weren't even looking!

What's the point in writing all of this down, since God knows your thoughts already? There are several points, really:

1. No conversation should be one-sided. This is your side.
2. Because writing comes naturally to you, you'll be able to focus on God much more easily than if you just tried to "think" your prayers.
3. After you've been doing it for a while, you'll find yourself writing down what you are "hearing" God say. That's the amazing way God works.

For Choice (B) People—The Talkers

- Find a quiet place where you can be alone on a regular basis. In some households that can be a challenge! But work at it, and pray about it, and something will emerge for you. Is there a tree you can climb? A corner of the garage you can curl up in? Is there a big walk-in closet in your parents' room you could close up in (with permission, of course)? Be creative if you have to—the tool shed, the bathtub, behind the boxes of Christmas decorations in the attic—but find a special private spot.
- Go there every day for about twenty minutes—longer if you can and you feel the urge to. Try to make it the same time everyday, so that it's as much

a part of your routine as eating and sleeping. That might mean making some sacrifices—maybe getting up twenty minutes earlier in the morning. It could mean rearranging your schedule—perhaps having your quiet time when you would usually be watching after-school cartoons with your brothers. It could even mean replacing some other activity—like yakking on the phone for twenty minutes with a friend you already hung out with all day!

• During the time between your visits to your private place, mentally collect things you want to talk to God about. You *can* write them down, but if that sounds like a chore to you, don't do it; just count on your memory. Gather in your mind the problems you want to discuss, the things you want to thank God personally for, the questions that have popped into your mind, the mistakes you'd like to get off your conscience, the people you want to talk to God about.

• When you go to your private place that same time every day with your mind teeming with conversation topics, get alone with God and start talking, girl! If it helps to imagine God sitting across from you, do that. If you find you talk more easily with your eyes closed, that's okay too. Talk about everything—pour it out as only you can—jabber until you run out of things to say. And then listen. Sometimes you'll feel as if God is answering you. Sometimes you'll just feel peaceful. Sometimes you'll feel unsettled—but that just means God's asking you to be patient, so don't worry. The point is, you've expressed your true self to God—and God loves that. It's what he wants most from you.

For Choice (C) People–The Doers

• Put together a God Scrapbook, just the way you'd create one to display the mementos of any other special friendship. It's a little more of a challenge, since you and God haven't squished into one of those photo booths at the mall and had your picture taken together! But give it some thought, and you'll come up with some fun ideas. What about special verses from the Bible that you feel God led you to? How about pictures of the people you know who seem close to God or who have helped you understand and love Jesus like your Sunday school teacher, youth pastor or Godmother? And what about markers for the milestones in your Christian journey? Do you have pictures of your baptism? A palm cross from Palm Sunday? The cross you wore as a baby? The program from the pageant where you got to play Mary?

You probably even have "souvenirs" that would mean nothing to anyone else, but that remind you of special times with God. Do you still have that lone flower that was growing up through the crack in the sidewalk that made you think that it's possible for God to help anybody bloom anywhere? Or the perfect four-leaf clover that always reminds you that God is perfect? The best thing about a God Scrapbook is that you can keep adding to it and then look back from time to time to see how much more God seems to be talking to you, now that you're noticing!

• Think about doing some special "routine" each time you have prayer time, which should be everyday. Would Mom let you light a candle that would burn while you prayed, symbolizing God's light right there beside you? Is there special music that lifts your heart and helps you feel God when you sing it? Could you play that and sing a verse or two before you pray each time? There are many traditions in the various denominations of the Christian faith that have helped Christians for centuries find their connection with God. They aren't *required*—it's not as if you can't get in touch with God without them—but they can be lovely ways to make your focused time with God rich and real. These include things like:

- a special cross you have nearby.
- folding your hands and bowing your head.
- making the sign of the cross with your hand from your head to your heart and across your chest.
- holding a Christian symbol in your hands while you pray.

Make something you ordinarily do a form of prayer in itself. Some artists think of God while they paint. There are musicians who offer every note to God when they play. Couldn't you make a dance a prayer—or a drawing, or a beautifully done report for school? You will find God entering into those projects and making them even more amazing than you could have done them alone.

For Choice (D) People—The Thinkers

- Like "The Talkers" you'll need to find a quiet place and time each day to really focus your thoughts on God. Since you won't actually be talking out loud, your place doesn't have to be quite as secluded, as long as you can count on no one interrupting you because they think you aren't "doing anything!"
- There are many ways to have silent conversations with God, but here is one suggestion that many Christians have found quite wonderful. Get into a comfortable position and close your eyes. Take a few deep breaths just to get the kinks out. Begin by silently asking God to be with you, to protect you from any thoughts that would separate you rather than bring you together. Ask God to bring you the thoughts he wants you to have about him. With your eyes still closed look at the darkness. Slowly,

images will form in your mind as you think about God. Pay attention to them. An image of a bridge might help you cross over all the every day stuff that keeps you from remembering God. An image of a heart may remind you how much God loves you.

- Then simply tell God, in your mind, what you're thinking. Listen. Do new thoughts come in that you need to follow? If not, just imagine God and the conversation you would love to have with him. He will put the right thoughts into your head because he knows you are really listening and you really want to hear and understand. Some people suddenly think of a Bible verse in the middle of such a conversation, something like, "Read about Jacob's ladder." They do—and the solution to a problem that's been bothering them suddenly becomes clear. There is no reason why simply having silent conversations with God won't do the same thing for you.

Girlz WANT TO KNOW

So far in talking about improving our God integrity, we've focused on how we can be *real* in our relationship with God. That's a huge part of it. But as we develop that relationship, issues can come up that test our integrity. If we want to stay whole and complete with God, we need to be prepared for those. That's why the Girlz want to know things like these.

✿ *LILY: I write to God in my Talking to God Journal every night, and it really helps. Only lately when I'm writing, I find out I'm asking questions like, "Are only certain people God's chosen people, like the Bible says? But, God, that doesn't seem quite fair. Shouldn't everybody have a chance?" Am I some kind of heathen or something for asking questions like that? Should I actually ask a person—you know—out loud? Or should I keep it to myself in my journal?*

What's happening in your journal, Lily, is exactly what *should* be happening! What safer place to come up with those kinds of questions than with God, who understands everything? And who's to say God didn't put those questions in your mind in the first place? We always learn best when we're having the questions that are the most important to us answered. So by all means, ask somebody! But make sure it's someone that meets these qualifications (this is not the time to strike up a conversation with that new boy in the class who, though cute, has never darkened the door of a church!). Make it:

- someone you admire as a Christian.
- an adult or at least a very mature older teen.
- somebody who doesn't just talk about the Bible, but who seems to really live his or her faith (walks the walk).
- somebody you feel comfortable talking to.
- somebody your parents would feel comfortable having you talk to (it could even BE one of your parents!).
- somebody you know who isn't going to be shocked that you would have the *nerve* to question something in the Bible.

If you feel your question has been answered in a way that gives you a peaceful feeling, write the answer down in your journal. If you're still unsettled, talk to someone else. It is *very* healthy for you to have questions and even healthier to search until God leads you to the right answer. You go, girl!

✿ *RENI: I'm one of those "doer" types, and I really do believe that I can feel God's pleasure when I'm playing my violin. It's like I'm praying when I'm making beautiful music. People have even said they can see it on my face. They don't see it on my face when I'm in church! Our worship services are so boring I want to scream. Half the time I can barely stay awake. I'm thinking of asking my parents if I can just stay at home and practice my music on Sunday mornings instead of going to church and being tortured. Do you think I should?*

You can always ask—but chances are your parents are going to say, "Uh-uh, Honey. Get yourself out of that bed." And they would be right. While playing the violin is your private way of having a personal relationship with God, there's more to spiritual integrity than just that. A huge part of it is how you share your experience with other believers. That means worshiping with them—having fellowship with them—watching everybody's kids grow up—rallying around when somebody's sick or in trouble—learning from each other. Your problem seems to be that those things aren't happening at your church, or you haven't noticed that they are. There are some things you could do to make that better:

- Offer to play your violin during a worship service as a special offering. You would not only be livening up the service, but you'd be sharing your experience with God with other people, just like he says we're supposed to.
- If the sermon is all that boring, spend that time looking around the church and making a mental list of how many people you like, people who have helped your family or who you have helped, or people who you've laughed with or shared dinner at a potluck supper with. Thank God for them. Later, thank *them*.
- Try to pick out one thing from the sermon that you can try during the week. You could even tell the pastor or someone else in the church and ask that person to hold you accountable. (If the sermon was about the Good Samaritan, for instance, ask them to hold you accountable for doing at least one good deed for an outcast kid at school during the week.)

If you were an adult, you could just find another church, but since that decision isn't under your control, go with what is. At the very least, remember that nobody was meant to worship God all by herself. Just that change in attitude is bound to improve things a little.

🌸 *SUZY: Since I haven't been going to church all that long, I don't know what's going on half the time. I would feel like a geek, though, if I were always raising my hand going, "What's being saved mean?" and "How do you surrender yourself to God?" Will I just kind of get it if I hang around long enough?*

You might, Suzy, but why walk around in a fog? There are several things you can do to get clear on what you're hearing.

1. Don't be afraid to ask questions. Christians who have gone to church all their lives sometimes tend to fall into the habit of using "jargon"—almost a code language—that sounds like a foreign language to newcomers to the faith. They need to be reminded to find fresh, clear ways to express their faith *and* you can bet you aren't the only one who doesn't understand just exactly what the Sam Hill they're talking about!

2. If you're really too shy to ask or if you *have* asked and somebody has said something like, "You don't even know *that*?" then carefully choose someone you can ask in private. What about the parents of whoever is taking you to church? How about the Sunday school teacher—after class? Does the pastor's wife seem like a cool lady—or how about the youth leader, even though you aren't old enough for youth group yet? Offer to buy a Coke for that person one afternoon after school and talk about some things you don't understand. Any Christian worth her salt is going to jump at the chance to help you.

3. Ask if you can borrow a simple translation of the Bible from the church library or the Sunday school room. There are Bibles put together just for kids your age (like the Young Women of Faith Bible) that you can read while curled up with a plate of cookies. These translations can clear up a lot of the phrases the "old-timers" toss around without even thinking.

4. Tell your close friends, the ones who have taken you to church, that the lingo is sometimes confusing. You'll be helping *them* make sure *they* know what they're talking about too!

ZOOEY: *I'm really getting into the whole church thing now. I even pray on my own, and I think I'm feeling happy more often than I did before. But there's one problem. In my Sunday school class, they say we're supposed to be, like, telling people who don't go to church all about Jesus and stuff. I would be so embarrassed to do that. Won't the kids at school think I'm a weirdo?*

There are some people—kids *and* adults—who think anybody who doesn't do things exactly the way they do is a weirdo, so that takes care of that one. If you're going to be a weirdo anyway, why not be one for God?

In fact, if you aren't willing to tell other people about how wonderful he is and how much better life is when you're connected to God, you aren't doing everything he's asking of you. It's on the assignment sheet of every Christian to spread the word.

So the real question is—how do you do it without feeling embarrassed? Here are some suggestions:

1. Remember that you don't have to preach a sermon or quote the Bible or hand out little pamphlets.
2. One of the best ways to spread Christianity is to *be* a good Christian and act like one all the time, 24/7. Then when someone asks, "How come you're happier than you used to be?" you can tell them.
3. You only have to be able to tell your own story. If people want to know more, invite them to church.
4. Talk about God when it's natural to. For example, if someone says, "Hey, Zooey, let me borrow your math homework," you can say, "No— I've learned from God that cheating isn't right. I'll be glad to help you, though." If you get a weird look or the person mutters, "Jesus freak," just say, "Thanks."
5. Do *not* join in when people are telling dirty jokes, making fun of Christians, gossiping about people, or being mean. If anybody asks why you're walking away, tell them—"This is *so* not a God thing."

Basically, you don't have to be Reverend Zooey—just be Christian Zooey. If your faith *is* your life, you won't be able to help sharing it.

Talking to God About It

Choose one of the suggestions under **Just Do It!** for this particular conversation with God. Pick the one that most appeals to you. As you do your activity, include the integrity issues from this list that seem to be calling your name, like:

- help with doubts.
- help with church boredom.
- help in understanding Christianity.
- freedom from being embarrassed about God.
- being really good instead of just *looking* like I'm good.
- being real with God.
- not being afraid of being considered a freak.
- finding the best way to connect with God.

If some kid wanted to know what I really think about God, I would …

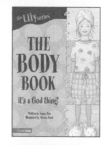

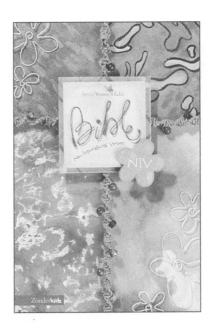

NIV Young Women of Faith Bible
General Editor Susie Shellenberger

Designed just for girls ages 8-12, the *NIV Young Women of Faith Bible* not only has a trendy, cool look, it's packed with fun to read in-text features that spark interest, provide insight, highlight key foundational portions of Scripture, and more. Discover how to apply God's word to your everyday life with the *NIV Young Women of Faith Bible*.

Hardcover 0-310-91394-2
Softcover 0-310-70278-X
Slate Leather–Look™ 0-310-70485-5
Periwinkle Leather–Look™ 0-310-70486-3

Available now at your local bookstore!

Zonderkidz.

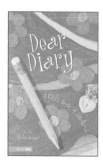

Now Available

Rough & Rugged Lily (Book 9)
Softcover 0-310-70260-7
The Year 'Round Holiday Book companion

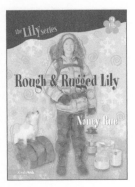

Lily Speaks! (Book 10)
Softcover 0-310-70262-3
The Values & Virtues Book companion

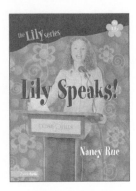

The Year 'Round Holiday Book ... It's a God Thing!
Softcover 0-310-70256-9
Rough & Rugged Lily companion

The Values & Virtues Book ... It's a God Thing!
Softcover 0-310-70257-7
Lily Speaks! companion

Zonder**kidz**.

We want to hear from you. Please send your comments about this
book to us in care of the address below. Thank you.

Zonder**kidz**.

Grand Rapids, MI 49530
www.zonderkidz.com